D1271298

WITHDRAWN
FROM THE
WILLIAMS UNIV.
LIBRARY

A HISTORY OF LANCASHIRE

Two historic bridges across the River Hodder. The near one, a Tudor bridge, is known as Cromwell's Bridge, presumably because he lodged at nearby Stonyhurst before and after the Battle of Preston, 1648. The far one, built by Macadam, was opened in 1826.

THE DARWEN COUNTY HISTORY SERIES

A History of Lancashire

J. J. BAGLEY

Cartography by D. H. BIRCH

PHILLIMORE

First published 1956
Second edition 1961
Third edition 1964
Fourth edition, revised and enlarged 1967
Fifth edition, revised and enlarged 1970

Sixth edition 1976
published by
PHILLIMORE & CO. LTD.,
London and Chichester

Head Office: Shopwyke Hall,
Chichester, Sussex, England

ISBN 0 85033 246 X

Printed in Great Britain by
UNWIN BROTHERS LIMITED
at The Gresham Press, Old Woking, Surrey

Contents

The Law Courts (Shire Hall), Lancaster Castle

Maps and Plans

Collegiate Church, Manchester

List of Plates

Acknowledgements

I am grateful to Norman Duerden for the frontispiece and plate 16; to Owen Ashmore for 1; to *Lancashire Life* for 2 and 8; to K. Wolstenholme for 4; to *The Guardian* for 5; to *The Times* for 6; to *The Southport Visiter* for 9 and 10; to Fred Quinn for 11, 12, 14, 20, 21 and 37; to C. F. Barber for 13; to Manchester Libraries Committee and to Harry Milligan for 22, 24, 25 and 28; to Picturepoint for 23; Kathleen Eyre for 39 and 41; to Atkinson Library, Southport for 40 and 42, and to Philip Garlick for 38, 43 and 44.

Plate 7 and the map of Widnes on page 96 are printed by permission of H. M. Stationery Office, Crown copyright reserved.

Thanks are also due to Kenneth Sanderson of Liverpool University for preparing the marginal drawings for printing.

Preface

During the last half century, and particularly since 1945, both the reading public and the professional historian have found increasing interest in local history. But without relation to the background of national history, local history tends to become a mere gathering together of facts without perspective or sense of values, instead of being a study which enriches and illustrates British and even European history. The purpose of this book, therefore, is to set the history of Lancashire into the background of British history, and to show how people living in the county were affected by such broad movements as the Reformation and the Industrial Revolution, and by such national events as the Civil Wars and Parliamentary Reform.

Entrance to Peel Hall, Little Hulton, the home of the Kenyon family

Lancashire is particularly fortunate in its local history resources. The student can find abundant manuscript material in the Lancashire Record Office at Preston, the John Rylands Library at Manchester, the city libraries of Manchester and Liverpool, the five Universities, and a score or so of borough libraries. Printed sources and interpretative articles he will find in the volumes of the five publishing societies, the Chetham Society, the Historic Society of Lancashire and Cheshire, the Record Society of Lancashire and Cheshire, the Lancashire and Cheshire Antiquarian Society, and the Lancashire Parish Register Society. The eight volumes of the *Victoria County History* rarely fail to provide facts or references helpful for the most detailed searches into the county's history.

Since my own researches into Lancashire history have been largely confined to the sixteenth and seventeenth centuries. I have had to use the work of many Lancashire scholars in making this wide survey. I have acknowledged their help in the bibliography.

In April 1974 Lancashire suffered partition. The two new metropolitan counties of Merseyside and Greater Manchester commandeered most of South Lancashire, Cumbria seized Cartmel and Furness, and even Cheshire crossed the Mersey to occupy Warrington and Widnes. Present-day administrative changes, however, cannot change centuries of history, so, for the purpose of this book, *Lancashire* still means what it has meant since the Middle Ages, when Roger of Poitou first brought the area under his rule and when Edward III first created the county palatine.

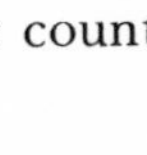

The University, Liverpool. J.J.B.

I Roman Lancashire

Ceremonial helmet found at Ribchester

The Romans began the conquest of Britain in 43 A.D., almost a century after Julius Caesar had first crossed the Channel from Gaul. Five years' fighting gave them control of most of the south-eastern half of Britain, and by 60 Suetonius Paulinus had carried the conquest as far as Chester and North Wales. But the Romans did not hold the south-east sufficiently strongly to justify so rapid an advance. The revolt of the Iceni under Queen Boudicca forced Suetonius Paulinus to rush his troops south again in order to defend London, and not until the 70s did the Romans attempt to conquer the backward Brigantes who occupied most of northern Britain. In the early days of the Conquest the Romans had found the Brigantes under their queen, Cartimandua, amenable and co-operative, but before 70 A.D. these early iron-age Britons had become hostile and troublesome. Between 71 and 74 the ninth legion built a fort at York (Eburacum) and pushed north-westward as far as Carlisle (Luguvallium). This campaign established Roman control north of Lancashire. In 78 Agricola brought the twentieth legion, Valeria Victrix, to Chester (Deva). After he had subdued the Ordovices in North Wales, he led his soldiers across the Mersey by the ford at Latchford, and marched north towards the Ribble and east towards the Pennines. He soon built earth ramparts to defend the small garrisons he left at Ribchester (Bremetennacum), Manchester (Mamucium), and Overborough (Galacum), and during the next three years his men constructed rough roads to link these forts to Carlisle, Ilkley (Olicana) and York. Agricola himself led the relentless march to the north. By 82 he was across the Tay, and in 84 he won the decisive battle of Mons Graupius against the Caledonians in the eastern highlands of Scotland.

So far the Romans had done little but march straight through the area we now call Lancashire. The Roman historian, Tacitus, son-in-law of Agricola, described how the Romans 'with sudden attacks and punishments' terrified the Brigantes. 'When Agricola had alarmed and terrified them sufficiently, he next tried the effects of good usage and the attractions of peace.' Certainly his officers forced the Brigantes into road-making and trench-digging. Everything was done to keep the advance going. But Agricola was recalled in 84, and under the Emperors Trajan (98-117) and Hadrian (117-138) the plan to conquer the northern highlands was abandoned. Hadrian's Wall (122-128)

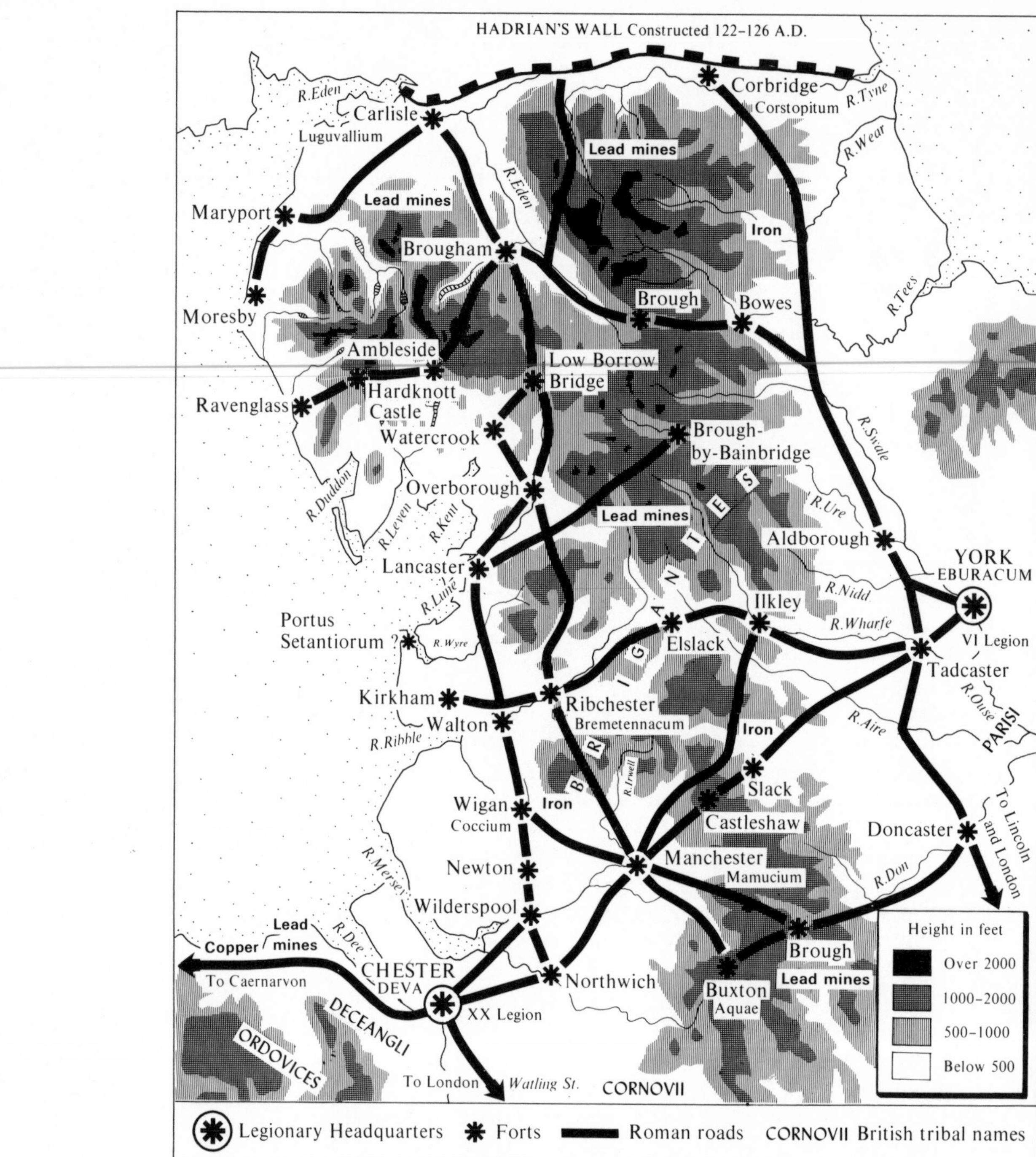

North West Britain *c.* 300 A.D.

eventually restricted the area of Roman occupation, and made it necessary to have safe and good roads leading to it from the legionary centres of Chester and York. Therefore during the first half of the second century the roads through Lancashire were increased in number and made more permanent. The old forts were made bigger and stronger, stone walls or timber palisades replaced earth ramparts, and additional strong points were built at Wilderspool, Wigan (Coccium), Walton-le-Dale, Kirkham, Lancaster, and possibly at Colne. This Roman consolidation and expansion at first prompted the Brigantes to resist whenever they could. It is recorded that Antoninus Pius, who succeeded Hadrian as emperor in 138, had to suppress a revolt in the north, but the Brigantes could do little against the military superiority of the Romans. To the Romans Lancashire was unattractive because of its climate and its distance from Europe, and there is little evidence that Roman civilians ever settled there. No sites of Roman villas have been found in Lancashire. Some ex-soldiers married local girls and stayed on to farm in the Ribble valley and probably in the neighbourhood of Mamucium. Some Roman traders may have lived for short periods in or near one of the bigger forts, but most Romans who came to Lancashire were active soldiers on defence duties. Once they had finished their tour of duty they moved elsewhere, and were no more permanent than British soldiers are to-day in Germany or Hongkong.

Samian Ware found in plenty at Walton-le-Dale

Lancashire is poor country for the archaeologist. Industrial development during the last three hundred years has destroyed or overbuilt much of the evidence the archaeologist would like to discover. New knowledge of the fort of Mamucium has been found under cellar floors of warehouses near Knott Mill station and by rescue digs when nearby property was rebuilt. At Walton-le-Dale excavation had to await the convenience of the market gardeners who occupied the site. The Roman sites at Lancaster, Wigan, Warrington, and Ribchester are thick with property. Even so, during the last hundred and fifty years some interesting Roman finds have been made. Inscribed altar-stones and tomb-stones have been found at Lancaster, Ribchester, Warrington and Manchester, and preserved in local museums. Various Roman coins and pieces of jewellery have been dug up, and the Walton site has yielded a large quantity of Samian ware, which is red glazed pottery imported from Europe. In 1796 an elaborately-carved bronze helmet was discovered at Ribchester, and last century there were unearthed a bronze statuette of Jupiter at Manchester, a bronze bust of Minerva at Warrington, part of a Roman altar at Wigan, and various stretches of the original gravel surface of Roman roads, usually about thirteen feet wide. Since 1945, there have been enlightening excavations at Lancaster, Manchester, Castleshaw, Walton, Kirkham, and Ribchester.

II *Anglo-Saxon Lancashire*

Anglian Cross with runes found at Lancaster

The Anglian Settlement

Archaeology has been able to discover little about the settlement of the Angles in Lancashire. Celtic writers are too vague and general to be of much help, and the Anglo-Saxon chroniclers, so informative about busier and more important areas, make few references to the area which became Lancashire. However, place-name and geographical evidence provides a reliable source of information, and fortunately this is strong enough to form a reasonably clear picture of what took place.

The Angles came into Lancashire from the east, from Yorkshire (Deira) and from Northumberland and Durham (Bernicia). About 570 A.D. small family groups began to cross the Pennines, and settle on fairly high ground in the Lune and Ribble valleys, and on isolated sites clear of the marshland on the coastal plain. The *inga* place-names shown on the map are of this early period. *Melling* is the place where the followers or family of Mealla settled; *Billinge,* an early name but not necessarily 'inga' in form, means either the home of Bylla's family, or the home of the people on the hill, or, simply the place on the hill. The *ingaham* names suggest a second wave of settlement about 600. Most likely both these settlements were peacefully made. But with King Ethelfrith of Bernicia, the conqueror of Deira, came war. He made two armed thrusts westwards. The first probably came down the Lune valley towards Morecambe Bay and ended in 603 with victory for the Angles at Degsaston, an undiscovered battle-site. The second crossed the Pennines further south, and drove through the Manchester area and across the Mersey before achieving a triumphant climax in the decisive defeat of the British at Chester in 615. A third wave of Anglian colonists followed on the heels of this military conquest. The *ingaton* names indicate some of their places of settlement. From that time until the eleventh century the Angle population in Lancashire steadily increased. It is not possible to say how many settlements they made. More than two hundred *tun* names of this later period have been identified with certainty, but many more must have been obliterated by Norse and Danish names in the following centuries.

It is hard to discover whether the Angle and Romano-British inhabitants of Lancashire lived peaceably together or not. Gildas, a

1. Anglian Cross, one of three (probably ninth century,) in Whalley churchyard.

2. Norse Cross, Halton (about 1000 A.D.). This panel shows the Christian symbols.

3. St. Peter's Church, Heysham, the younger of the two pre-Norman foundations on this site sacred to early Christians.

4. Cartmel Priory Church: founded in the twelfth century but largely rebuilt in the fifteenth.

5. Whalley Abbey: the North West Gateway, built early in the fourteenth century.

6. Furness Abbey: looking east along the twelfth-century nave towards the high altar.

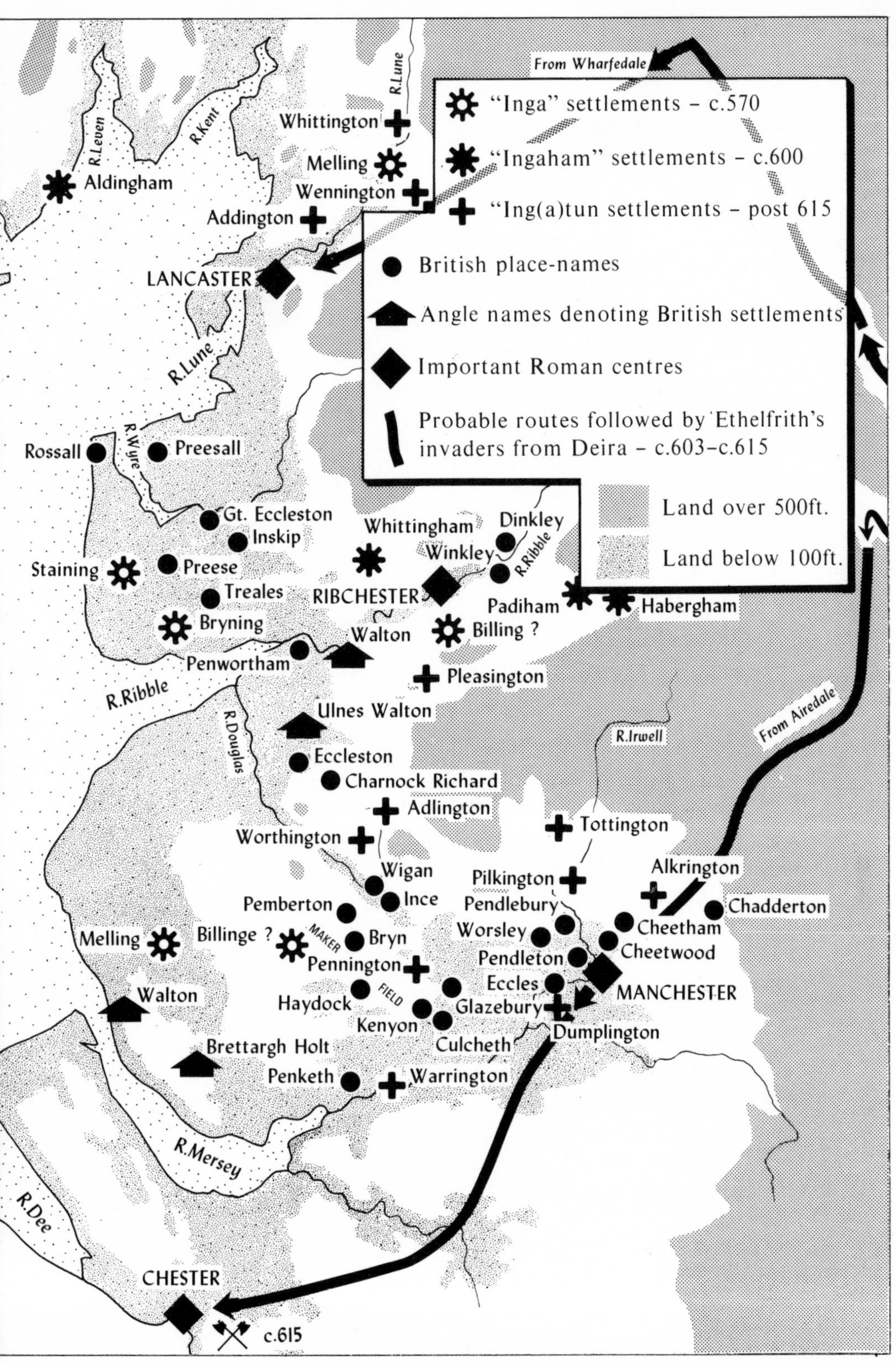
From Wharfedale
"Inga" settlements – c.570
"Ingaham" settlements – c.600
"Ing(a)tun settlements – post 615
British place-names
Angle names denoting British settlements
Important Roman centres
Probable routes followed by Ethelfrith's invaders from Deira – c.603–c.615
Land over 500ft.
Land below 100ft.
R.Leven
R.Kent
R.Lune
Whittington
Melling
Wennington
Aldingham
Addington
LANCASTER
R.Lune
R.Wyre
Rossall
Preesall
Gt. Eccleston
Inskip
Whittingham
Dinkley
Winkley
R.Ribble
Staining
Preese
Treales
RIBCHESTER
Padiham
Habergham
Bryning
Walton
Billing ?
Penwortham
Pleasington
R.Ribble
Ulnes Walton
R.Douglas
R.Irwell
From Airedale
Eccleston
Charnock Richard
Adlington
Tottington
Worthington
Wigan
Pilkington
Alkrington
Ince
Pemberton
Pendlebury
Chadderton
Melling
Billinge ?
MAKER
Bryn
Worsley
Cheetham
Cheetwood
Pennington
Pendleton
Eccles
MANCHESTER
Walton
Haydock
FIELD
Glazebury
Kenyon
Dumplington
Culcheth
Brettargh Holt
Penketh
Warrington
R.Mersey
R.Dee
CHESTER
c.615

Anglian Settlement of Lancashire

Arms of Whalley Abbey. Whalley was an important ecclesiastical centre in Anglo-Saxon times

Celtic writer, described the Anglian invasion as 'a fire from the East which burned from sea to sea' and 'did not die down until, consuming almost all the island that stood above ground, it licked the Western Ocean with its red and savage tongue'. Even Bede the Anglian historian wrote of Ethelfrith's conquest as ruthless, and told how the Angles viciously attacked a large group of non-combatant priests who accompanied the British soldiers at Chester. On the other hand certain facts suggest that the Angles at least tolerated the Britons. Some codes of Anglo-Saxon law gave the British a lowly but recognised standing; some Angles of leading families were given British personal names, a fact which suggests intermarriage between Angles and British; and the revival of Celtic art after the Anglian invasion shows that British craftsmen were able and probably encouraged to continue with their work.

In Lancashire more than fifty British place-names have survived. Almost all of them are found south of the Ribble, centred round Wigan and Manchester. There are none at all in the Lune valley which the Angles made a principal area of settlement, and, with the exception of Ince Blundell, none in the coastal area of south Lancashire, which the Norse later occupied in force. *Wigan* is derived from a British personal name, *Treales* from a British habitation name, and *Makerfield* from a British district name, but most of the others are topographical names, embodying such British words as *pen* (hill), *cet* (wood), *ince* (island in the marsh), *ecles* (church) or *cader* (hill-fort). These topographical names were often accepted by the Angles, not always with full understanding of the meaning of the British word. Thus to *pen* they added their own name for *hill* to produce Pendle, and later generations even added a third *hill* to give us *Pendle Hill.* Similarly to *cet* was added *wood* to give *Cheetwood,* now an area of Manchester. The Angles and Norse distinguished isolated British communities with such names as *Walton, Ulnes Walton* and *Brettargh Holt*. In those areas there could not have been other British settlements, or else such a designation as *Walton,* 'the settlement of the British', would have had no point.

The Celtic Britons could not prevent the English from steadily making themselves masters of the area between the Mersey and Morecambe Bay, even though they managed eventually to convert their new masters to Christianity. By 900 English control was strong enough to subdue the many new Scandinavian settlements in the area.

Apart from several small finds of Anglo-Saxon coins, three hoards have been found in Lancashire; one at Little Crosby near Liverpool in 1611, one on Halton Moor near Lancaster in 1815, and one at Cuerdale near Preston in 1840. The last contained no less than ten thousand silver coins and almost a thousand ounces of silver ingots, all packed into a leaden chest. The treasure is thought to have been hidden away by the Danish army in its flight before Edward the Elder in 911. Most of the coins were Danish and had been minted at York, but among them were almost a thousand coins of Alfred the Great and about fifty of Edward the Elder.

Danes and Norsemen

The seventh century was the golden age of Northumbria. Originally consisting of two independent kingdoms, Bernicia and Deira, it was united in 605, and during the reign of Edwin expanded into the most powerful of the Anglo-Saxon kingdoms. It stretched from the Humber to the Forth and the western coast and included the isles of Anglesey and Man. But in the following century Mercia replaced it as the most important English kingdom, although Northumbria continued for some time as a principal seat of learning and literary activity. In the ninth century the leadership of the English passed from Mercia to the kingdom of Wessex.

Therefore on Wessex fell the heaviest burden of organising resistance against the Danish invasions, which began with isolated raids on the east and south coasts of England in the later years of the eighth century, but which developed into damaging campaigns inland during the next hundred years. In 865 the Great Army of the Danes landed in East Anglia intent on beginning a permanent conquest of England. By 874 the king of Mercia had been driven into exile, and in eastern Mercia—the present-day Derbyshire, Leicester and Northamptonshire—the Danes were already establishing settlements. Most of south-western Northumbria (i.e. Lancashire) escaped these devastating attacks, but place-names in the Manchester area, such as Hulme, Oldham (Aldhulme), Flixton, Urmston, and Hulme near Winwick, reveal the north-western fringe of Danish settlement. The track of this invasion can be traced back through eastern Cheshire in such place-names as Cheadle Hulme, Holmes Chapel, Hulme Walfield, Kettleshulme, Knutsford and Toft.

About 900, however, the western coast of Northumbria and the north-western coast of Mercia were invaded by many boatloads of Norsemen, who sailed from northern Ireland and the Isle of Man. The forefathers of these invaders had journeyed from Scandinavia round the north of Scotland to find new homes in the Western Isles and in Ireland. Many had become Christians. To Lancashire these Norsemen appear to have come as fairly peaceful settlers. The position of their homesteads and the evidence from *Domesday Book* (see page 25) suggest that they were soon living as friendly neighbours with the Angles, and often were content to farm inferior land.

'Across the Sands'. Many Norse families settled north of Morecambe Bay

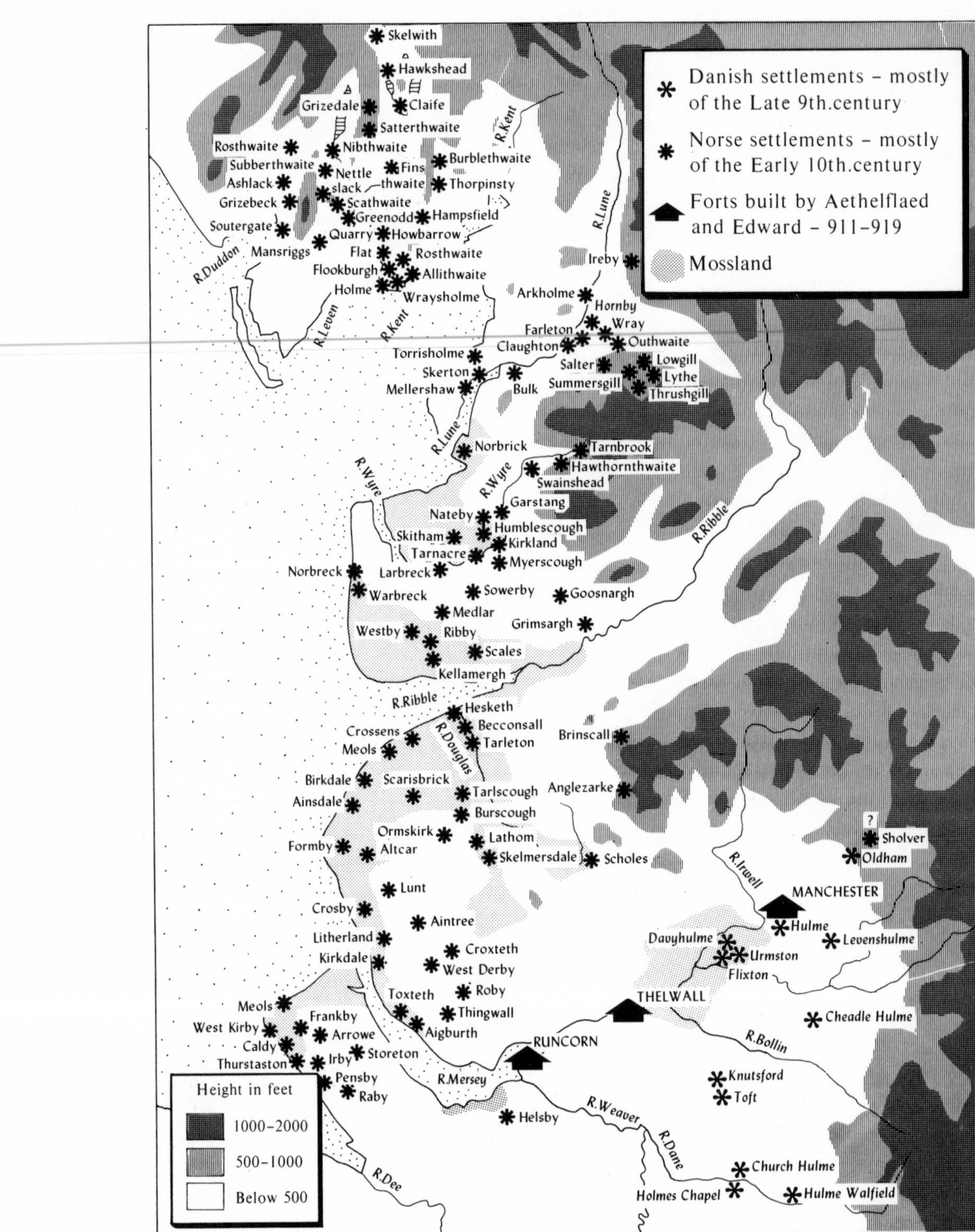

Norse and Danish Settlement

Undoubtedly there were occasional skirmishes especially in the early stages of the settlement, but the Norse filtered into Lancashire rather than invaded it. Their language came to be dominant in many districts of the area for several generations. For years after the Norman Conquest Lancashire men were measuring land not in Anglian hides and yardlands, but in Norse carucates (or ploughlands) and bovates (or oxgangs), and reckoning values not by the English silver penny but by the Norse ora. Even as late as the twelfth and thirteenth centuries many a Lancashire boy was christened Stainulf or Thurstan or Siward as his Norse ancestors had been.

'Loaves and fishes' cross (Irish-Norse) found at Hornby

Norse and Danish place-names often look alike. *Kir(k)by* or *Ormskirk* could be either Norse or Danish in origin. But so many place-names in western Lancashire have distinctive Norse characteristics that it is not difficult to show that this extensive Scandinavian settlement was Norse and not Danish. There is no doubt about place-names such as Scarisbrick, Norbreck, Lowgill, Brinscall, Scales, Ashlack or Nettleslack, and some place-names, such as Goosnargh, Grimsargh, Anglezarke and Becconsall, are even partly Irish as well as partly Norse.

After the death of Alfred the Great the defence of England fell chiefly on the shoulders of two of Alfred's children, Edward the Elder, the new king of Wessex, and Aethelflaed, Lady of the Mercians. Brother and sister built a series of defensive forts. The fort at Runcorn, situated at the base of the present Runcorn railway bridge, itself called after Aethelflaed, guarded the Mersey at one of its narrowest points. In 919, the year after Aethelflaed's death, Edward built forts at Thelwall and at Manchester to strengthen the English position in the Mersey valley, and eventually forced the Norse army in Yorkshire to surrender. Aethelstan, his son, did even better. He carried the fight north of the Ribble, and in 937 at the battle of Brunanburgh, the site of which is still unknown, he defeated an important coalition of his enemies, and was everywhere acknowledged as king of the English. Brunanburgh marked the beginning of a most welcome period of peace, which lasted until 980. Then a new series of Danish attacks, which culminated in Canute's conquest of England, renewed the struggle.

Until the days of Edward the Elder and Aethelstan, the Mersey had been the boundary between the kingdoms of Mercia and Northumbria. But in the general settlement after Brunanburgh, the Ribble became the new southern limit of Northumbria, and the land between the Ribble and the Mersey passed into the hands of the king. He kept it separate from Mercia, and in the following century it did not become part of the earldom of Mercia. It remained as a royal domain until after the Norman Conquest.

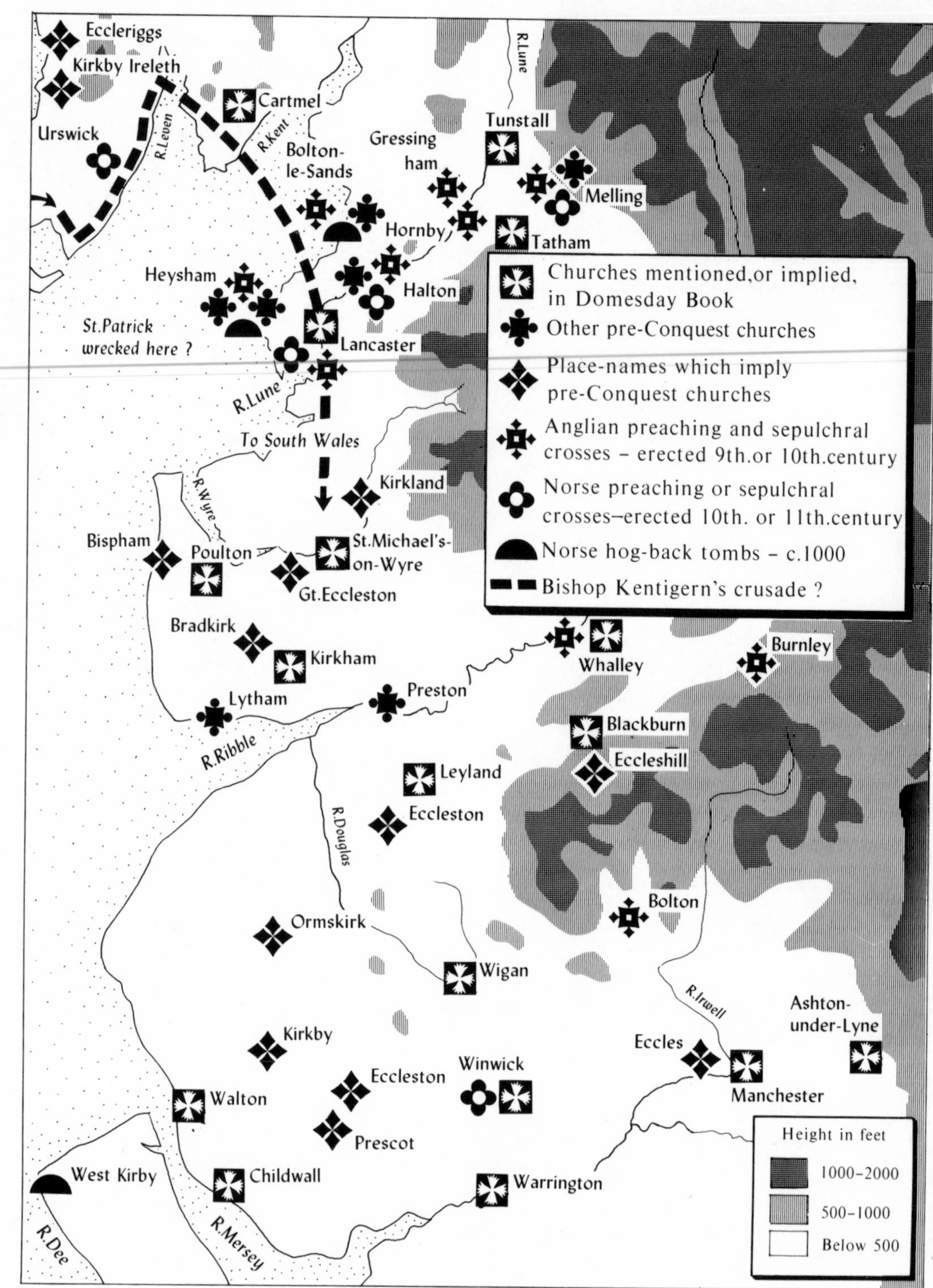

Eccleriggs
Kirkby Ireleth
Urswick
R.Leven
Cartmel
R.Kent
Bolton-le-Sands
Gressingham
R.Lune
Tunstall
Melling
Hornby
Tatham
Heysham
Halton
St.Patrick wrecked here ?
Lancaster
R.Lune
To South Wales
R.Wyre
Kirkland
Bispham
Poulton
St.Michael's-on-Wyre
Gt.Eccleston
Bradkirk
Kirkham
Lytham
Preston
R.Ribble
Whalley
Burnley
Blackburn
Eccleshill
Leyland
Eccleston
R.Douglas
Ormskirk
Bolton
Wigan
R.Irwell
Ashton-under-Lyne
Kirkby
Eccles
Manchester
Winwick
Eccleston
Walton
Prescot
West Kirby
Childwall
Warrington
R.Dee
R.Mersey
Churches mentioned, or implied, in Domesday Book
Other pre-Conquest churches
Place-names which imply pre-Conquest churches
Anglian preaching and sepulchral crosses – erected 9th. or 10th. century
Norse preaching or sepulchral crosses – erected 10th. or 11th. century
Norse hog-back tombs – c.1000
Bishop Kentigern's crusade ?
Height in feet
1000–2000
500–1000
Below 500

The Coming of Christianity

The Coming of Christianity

The Christian gospel reached Britain well before the last century of the Roman occupation; but, with the exception of two Roman coins bearing Christian symbols, archaeologists so far have found nothing to suggest that there could have been Christian communities as early as this in the area we now call Lancashire. On the other hand there are several reasons for believing that soon after the departure of the Romans, Christian missionaries began to convert the native Romano-Britons, and, later, the Anglian settlers who crossed the Pennines from Deira. First, there is a persistent legend that St. Patrick (*c.* 389–461) was once wrecked off the shore of Morecambe Bay. Legend can be most misleading, but today on a cliff-head at Heysham still stand the ruins of St. Patrick's Chapel, built by the Angles probably before the year 800. Hard by St. Patrick's Chapel the Angles built a second church dedicated to St. Peter, a striking proof that the early Christians held this site particularly sacred. Secondly, about 1200 one of the monks of Furness Abbey recorded that, in the middle of the sixth century, Bishop Kentigern of Glasgow had led a Christian crusade from Cumberland to Wales mostly along the seashore, a journey which must have taken him into dozens of west Lancashire settlements. Thirdly, in the second half of the seventh century, Bishop Wilfrid of Ripon wrote not only of 'those holy places in divers regions which the British clergy had deserted' in the face of the Anglian invasion, but also of the lands and buildings in the Ribble valley and in Cartmel, which kings of Northumbria had presented to the Church. Fourthly, the presence of the British word *ēcles,* a church, in such place-names as Eccles and Eccleston, suggest the existence of Christian communities before, or at least in the early stages of, the Anglian settlement. Moreover, there is the evidence of the dedication to Anglian saints of at least five pre-Conquest churches (at Winwick, Poulton-le-Fylde, Lytham, Preston and Halton in the Lune valley), and the existence of Anglian crosses at Whalley, Lancaster, Bolton and other places, all of which strengthens the impression that there was a lively Christian Church working in Lancashire at least as early as the seventh and eighth centuries.

Carving and Runes on the Urswick cross

Irish Christians, the followers of St. Columba and St. Aidan, were the pioneer missionaries of this Church, but after the Synod of Whitby in 663 Celtic and Roman Christians joined forces. York became the administrative centre of the Northumbrian church, but when Aethelstan seized the land between the Ribble and the Mersey, he transferred his conquest into the Mercian diocese of Lichfield. There it remained until the creation of Chester diocese in 1541, but the church in northern Lancashire continued to be administered from York.

The Norse settlers who swarmed into Lancashire about 900 have left behind them evidences of their Christian activity. As the Angles did before them, they too marked their sacred places with stone crosses. A Norse cross can usually be recognised by its chain-pattern decorations, its carved snakes and dragons, and its wheel-head, or circle of stone running between the arms of the cross. Good examples of Norse stone crosses, now weather-worn and broken, can be seen at Winwick, Lancaster, Halton and Urswick; and at Heysham and Bolton-le-Sands still remain crudely-decorated stone Norse tombs known as hogbacks. These date from about the year 1000.

Christianity did not entirely drive out the old pagan beliefs. On the cross at Halton one side of the cross-shaft carries a sculptured representation of the Ascension of Christ, but the opposite side unmistakably depicts the pagan story of Sigurd the Volsung. Small stone crosses were used for marking important graves, but a preaching cross proclaimed a customary place of worship until labour and materials were available to build a church on the site. The investigators who compiled *Domesday Book* in 1086 mentioned fifteen churches in Lancashire, and referred indirectly to two others. In the north they recorded churches at Tatham and Tunstall and implied that there were churches at Cartmel and at [Kirk] Lancaster. In Amounderness they stated there were three churches, probably Kirkham, Poulton and St. Michael-on-Wyre. South of the Ribble they named churches at Blackburn, at Walton, St. Mary's at Whalley, St. Mary's at Manchester, St. Michael's at Ashton-under-Lyne, St. Oswald's at Winwick, St. Elfin's at Warrington, and the 'church of the manor' of Newton wapentake, which was probably Wigan church. They also spoke of priests holding land both at Childwall and in Leyland wapentake. But since the investigators did not set out to record churches, their list is incomplete. It does not include the churches at Preston, Lytham, Melling, Halton, Bolton-le-Sands and Heysham, which certainly were then in existence, nor those at such places as Ormskirk, Garstang, Sefton, Eccles and Prescot, which were probably pre-Conquest in origin.

Carving on one side of the Heysham hogback. Does this side represent the Resurrection?

III Domesday Survey and Lancashire

Wigan Parish Church—in Domesday Survey 'the church of the manor' in Newton wapentake?

Twenty years after the battle of Hastings, William the Conqueror held a detailed enquiry into the way in which land was owned and taxed in his new kingdom. He sent out officials into all parts of England except the most northerly areas to ask questions about the extent of land under the plough, the number of plough-teams, mills and fishponds, and to record the owners and value of all estates both in 1066 and 1086, the year in which the enquiry was being made. This information, arranged by counties, was recorded in two volumes of *Domesday Book,* nearly 1,700 pages all told. *Lancashire* does not appear because the county did not then exist as an administrative unit, but the one and a half pages concluding the description of Cheshire are headed *Between the Ribble and the Mersey,* and the parts of Lancashire north of the Ribble are included in the Yorkshire section. The detail given is patchy and at times difficult to understand, but these three pages of Latin, with their abbreviations and strangely-spelt names, are the earliest surviving description of the land between the Mersey and the Cumbrian hills.

At the time of the Conquest the royal estate between the Mersey and the Ribble was divided into six unequal divisions called wapentakes by the Norse settlers, and hundreds by the English. Each wapentake took its name from the royal manor within its border. The king's reeve farmed the manor lands. The rest he divided into small estates or berewicks, to be farmed by thanes, drengs or freemen, who paid rent to the king partly in money and partly in service. In Newton wapentake fifteen drengs farmed berewicks. Each dreng paid the king two shillings rent a year in addition to his customary services. In Warrington wapentake there were thirty-four drengs; in West Derby, sixty-five thanes, and in Salford, twenty-one; and in Blackburn, twenty-eight freemen, and in Leyland, twelve. These royal tenants each farmed two or three carucates of land. A carucate was equal to eight bovates or oxgangs, and, in Lancashire though not elsewhere, six carucates constituted one hide. It is not possible to give the equivalent of these measures in acres. Originally a bovate was the area of land which one ox could plough each year, probably about fifteen acres, but by 1086 all these measures seem to have become tax-assessment figures only. The different names by which the tenants were known probably indicated different services and duties, for thanes, freemen and drengs seem to have possessed

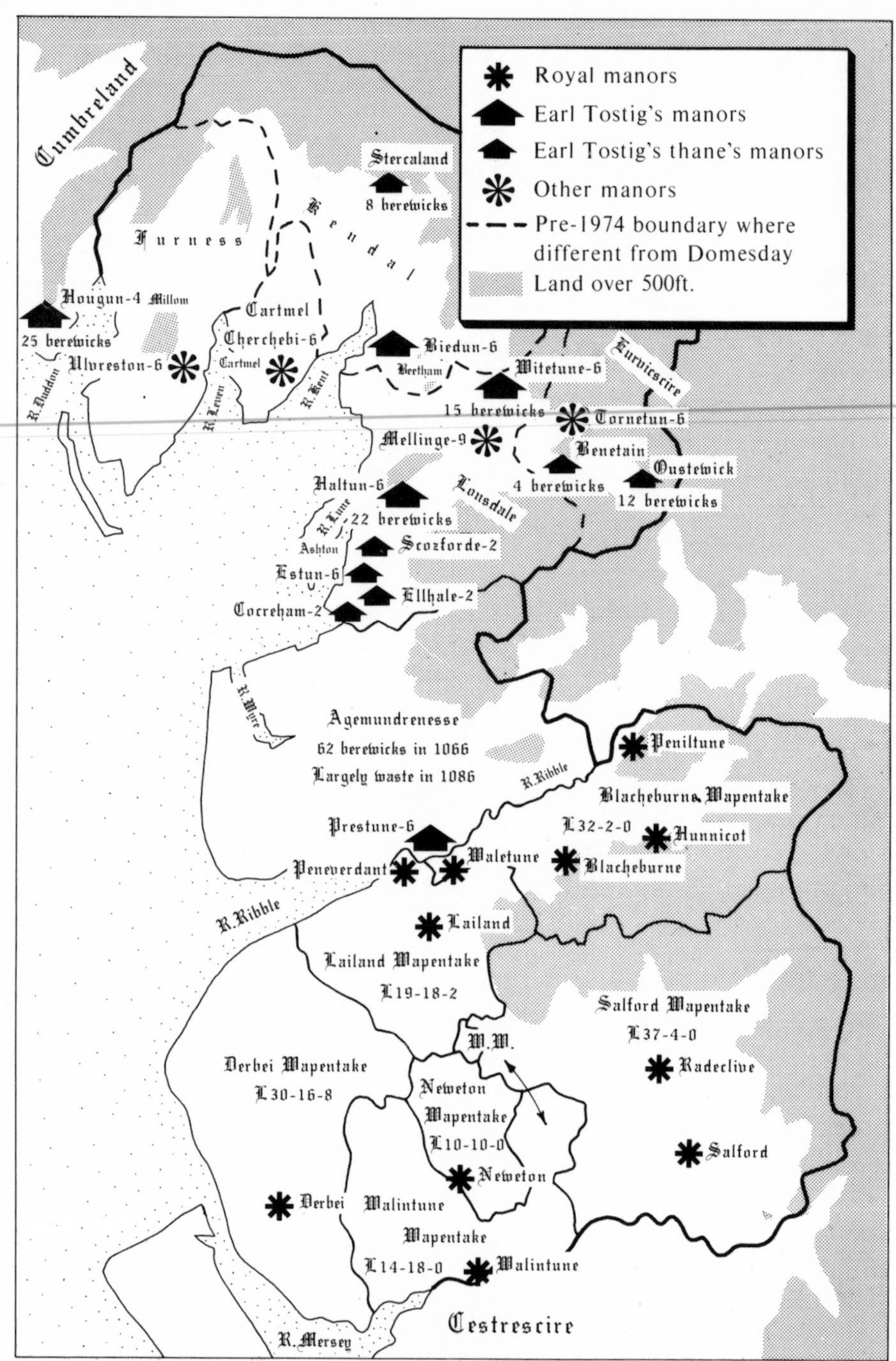

Domesday Survey

With the exception of *Furness*, *Cartmel*, *Kendal* and *Lonsdale*, the spelling of all names is that given in *Domesday Book.* Figures under each Wapentake south of the Ribble indicate the annual tax assessment in 1066. North of the Ribble, figures in brackets show the tax assessment of the domain lands of each manor measured in carucates in 1066. Kendal later became part of Westmorland and eastern Lonsdale part of Yorkshire.

equivalent social status. Lower down the social scale there were villeins, bordars or cotters, and serfs.

Domesday Book paints a picture of south Lancashire as an area of woodland and mosses, in which relatively small patches of land had been cleared and cultivated. Many thousands of acres were described as *waste* and the plentiful *pasture* was probably very rough grassland. There were no towns at all. People lived in scattered farmsteads or groups of cottages, and there could hardly have been ten thousand inhabitants in the whole area between the Ribble and the Mersey. Today twice ten thousand spectators are considered to be a poor 'gate' for a first-class football match. The land north of the Ribble was divided into two extensive wapentakes, Amounderness, centred upon the manor of Preston, and 'the king's land in Eurvicscire (Yorkshire)', which included the areas later known as Lonsdale, Kendal, Cartmel and Furness. Before 1066 these lands had belonged to an English noble, Earl Tostig, whom his brother, King Harold, defeated at Stamford Bridge a few days before the battle of Hastings. Within five years this northern area had suffered two ruthless invasions, the one in 1065-6 by Tostig's English enemies, and the other in 1069 when the Normans 'harried the north' as a punishment for revolt. *Domesday Book* records that in 1086 only sixteen of the sixty-two berewicks in Amounderness were inhabited, and it gives the impression that Lonsdale was a stricken and impoverished land. The area south of the Ribble could count itself fortunate. In 1086 its estates were assessed at £120 a year, a mere £25 less than their value in the days of Edward the Confessor.

Warrington Parish Church dedicated, according to Domesday Survey, to St. Elfin

Six or seven years after the Conquest, King William gave the land between the Ribble and the Mersey together with Amounderness to young Roger of Poitou, third son of that outstanding Norman baron, Roger Montgomery, earl of Shrewsbury. In the early 1090s William Rufus added Lonsdale, Cartmel and Furness to Roger's estates. In his turn Roger rewarded his most eminent supporters with baronies, for which they paid him military service. Not all the sub-tenants mentioned in *Domesday Book* can be identified with certainty, but Albert Grelley and Roger de Busli divided Blackburn wapentake between them; William FitzNigel held the barony of Widnes, and Roger de Montbegon received land north and south of the Ribble. Roger of Poitou chose Lancaster as the site for the castle from which he could administer and defend these estates. This was the beginning of the county of Lancaster, and in conjunction with the route over the Sands, explains why Furness and Cartmel, which geographically form a unit with Cumberland and Westmorland, were included within the borders of Lancashire.

IV Monks and Friars in Medieval Lancashire

There was probably not a single monastic house in Lancashire before the Norman Conquest. Since the number of monastic houses was a rough indication of an area's prosperity in pre-Conquest times, that striking fact is further proof of the sparse population, poverty and remoteness of this western part of the Northumbrian kingdom.

In 1094 Roger of Poitou encouraged the abbot of the Benedictine abbey of St. Martin at Séez in Normandy to send a dozen monks to found a daughter house at Lancaster. Roger endowed this priory handsomely. He gave it part of the township of Lancaster, several small estates in Lonsdale and Amounderness, and the revenues of a dozen churches in Lancashire and the Midlands. In the following century the abbey of Evesham and the priory of Durham, both Benedictine foundations, respectively inherited land in Penwortham and Lytham. Each built a tiny house on its estate for the two or three monks whom it sent to act as estate managers. In 1319 the priory of St. John at Pontefract founded a daughter house at Up Holland, near Wigan, with a prior and twelve monks. These four foundations, all of them minor ones, constituted a very small percentage of the two hundred and thirty houses which the Benedictines founded in England before the Reformation.

Lancashire's thinly populated areas were much more attractive to the Cistercians, the white monks, who wished to find in isolation and in manual work a stricter and more exacting way of life than the Benedictines led. They built in Lancashire two abbeys, Furness and Whalley, the ruins of which clearly show what large communities they must have housed. Furness, founded in the 1120s, held extensive lands, and the abbot was responsible for sheep-farming, turf-cutting and iron-smelting on the abbey's estates, as well as for frequently raising armed opposition against Scottish raiders. Whalley was a late foundation. Thanks to the patronage of the powerful de Lacy family of Clitheroe, the monks of Stanlow Abbey, Cheshire, first moved to Whalley in 1296. For the next 240 years they drew a very satisfactory income from the tithes of the parishes of Whalley, Blackburn, Eccles and Rochdale and from tenants who raised sheep and cattle on the abbey's lands.

Two orders of canons built houses in Lancashire. The Augustinians built four: Conishead (*c.* 1180), Burscough (*c.* 1190), Cartmel (*c.*1190), and Cockerham (*c.* 1207) Priories. The Premonstratensians built two, both *c.* 1180, a little priory at Hornby, and a large abbey on a lonely site at Cockersand overlooking the Lune estuary. The ruined chapter-house, with a modern roof, is all that remains of Cockersand today. Originally canons were secular priests whose chief work was to minister to the needs of the parishioners, but by the time these Lancashire houses were founded both orders of canons had many houses of regulars who followed a monastic Rule.

Chapter House, Furness Abbey

In the thirteenth century the friars came to England to foster a religious revival by preaching the Gospel and living lives of poverty and self-sacrifice. They founded their houses and churches in busy centres, because they had to live among people and not isolated from them. In Lancashire the Franciscans or Grey Friars built at Preston, the Dominicans or Black Friars at Lancaster, and the Austin or Augustinian Friars at Warrington.

The impression of a relatively poor medieval Lancashire, which this none too impressive catalogue of religious houses gives, is confirmed by the details of their landed possessions. Only Furness, Whalley and Cockersand can be held to have been major foundations, and Furness was easily the richest of the three. In 1535, the last full year before the beginning of the dissolution of the houses, Furness's net income was just over £800, a sizeable sum, but £300 less than the income of Fountains Abbey, and of course not comparable with some of the richest English abbeys, such as Glastonbury with a net income of £3,300, or St. Albans with £2,100. Whalley Abbey had a gross income of £550, but it had to spend a full £200 a year on the stipends of the vicars of its four dependent churches and on fees for its temporal officers. Cockersand's net income in its final year was a little less than £300, and incomes of the other Lancashire houses ranged from £100 or so enjoyed by Cartmel and Cockerham to the £18 a year which maintained Kersal Cell, a small religious centre outside Manchester, belonging to the priory of Lenton near Nottingham. *The Chartulary of Cockersand Abbey,* published by the Chetham Society in volumes 38–40, 43, 56–7, and 64 of the new series, shows from what numerous and scattered lands even a modest monastic income had often to be derived, and *The Act Book of the Ecclesiastical Court of Whalley* (Chetham Society, volume 44, new series) gives some idea of the many ways in which the bigger foundations touched the secular life of the area in which they were situated.

Warrington Friary from a sixteenth-century estate plan

The number of religious at each house was nothing like the same from generation to generation. In 1381, for example, Furness had twenty-three monks and Whalley twenty-four, but by the time of the

Dissolution the number at Furness had increased to thirty-nine and at Whalley had declined to thirteen. Up Holland Priory had difficulty in keeping at full strength. At the Dissolution it had five monks only. Cockersand usually had a score of canons; Cartmel, Burscough and Conishead had about half as many. Lancaster's full complement was one prior and eight monks, with two secular priests to serve the parish, and none of the other Lancashire houses had more than two or three monks in residence at a time. But it must be remembered that these figures take no account of lay brothers, secular officers and servants. The numbers of these varied considerably. The Cistercian houses usually employed most, but all houses which owned scattered lands needed agents to administer them and tenants to farm them.

Lancaster Priory was one of the alien priories of England, in that it had been founded by an abbey in Normandy. In Norman times there had been nothing strange or unusual about this, but after the loss of Normandy in 1204, the crown insisted that it should be consulted before a new prior was chosen or an existing prior expelled. At the beginning of the Hundred Years War, Edward III used the excuse of his quarrel with Philip of Valois to seize the possessions of all alien priories, and in 1414 Parliament officially transferred their estates to the permanent possession of the crown. It was one of the earliest signs of nationalist feelings beginning to affect ecclesiastical matters, and, in spirit at least, was kin to contemporary Lollardy. In 1415 Henry V handed over Lancaster's possessions to the new Bridgettine abbey of Syon which he was founding at Isleworth. The last prior of Lancaster was allowed to live out his life in office, and in 1430 a perpetual vicarage was established in the priory church. But until the Dissolution the abbess and convent of Syon could use as they wished the revenues, which each year their agents gathered from the lands which had originally belonged to Lancaster Priory.

Tower, rebuilt in 1754, of the Priory Church, Lancaster

The Pilgrimage of Grace, the northern protest movement sparked off by the Dissolution of the Lesser Monasteries in 1536, complicated the end of the Lancashire monasteries. Four canons and ten villagers from Cartmel were found guilty of rebellion and hanged. As early as March 1537, Whalley Abbey, unaffected by the Act of 1536, was 'taken into the king's hand' and its abbot, John Paslew, hanged because it had sheltered and fed some rebels. And, a month later, Abbot Pyle and his monks voluntarily surrendered Furness Abbey to the Crown when they realised that monasteries which belonged to international Orders had no place in the new, national church. The surrender of Furness was the beginning of the Dissolution of Greater Monasteries in the rest of the kingdom.

V The Lords of Lancaster, 1066-1322

Clitheroe Castle on site of Roger's motte and bailey

About 1072, after the 1069 rebellion in the north had been mercilessly suppressed, William the Conqueror added Amounderness and the land between the Ribble and the Mersey to other lands already possessed by young Roger of Poitou. By 1086, for reasons that are not clear, the crown had resumed administration of the land between the Ribble and the Mersey, but a few years later, as part of his plan for strengthening the north-west against the Scots, the new king, William Rufus, united under Roger's control Furness, Cartmel, Lonsdale, Amounderness and the land between the Ribble and the Mersey. Since the main invasion route from Scotland came round the Cumberland coast and across the sands of Morecambe Bay, it was logical to give the lord of Lancaster control of Cartmel and Furness, and to put Kendal in other hands, those of Ivo Taillebois. Roger did his military work well. By 1092 Rufus's forces controlled the border country round Solway Firth, and to consolidate their position were building Carlisle Castle. Roger was also giving some unity to the future county, Lancashire, by building a castle and priory at Lancaster, and by creating military fiefs such as the baronies of Manchester, Warrington, Penwortham and Widnes. But this unity was still very fragile. The honour of Lancaster which Roger possessed included several estates in other parts of England, and the old Northumbrian border along the Ribble valley still had much meaning for many northerners including the Scots.

In 1102 Roger supported his brother, Robert of Bellême, in an unsuccessful rebellion against Henry I. All his English estates were declared confiscate, and Henry granted the honour of Lancaster to Stephen of Blois, the grandson of the Conqueror. After Henry I's death in 1135 Stephen disputed the throne with Henry's daughter, Matilda. Naturally David of Scotland could not let slip the opportunities of gain offered by a divided England, and in 1139 he wrung from Stephen the promise to invest his son, Henry, with the earldom of Northumbria. Henry conveniently interpreted *earldom of Northumbria* to mean the old Saxon kingdom of Northumbria, and promptly brought his Scottish troops as far south as the Ribble. To add to the confusion, Ranulf II, earl of Chester, occupied the land between the Ribble and the Mersey, and then, negotiating first with Stephen's enemies and then with Stephen himself, tried to secure for

Lancaster's Borough Seal (obverse)

himself legal possession of the honour of Lancaster. He was temporarily successful, but in the general settlement reached in 1153 Stephen and Henry of Anjou, the future Henry II, agreed that Stephen's son William, soon to be count of Mortain, should hold the honour of Lancaster. In 1157 the Scots were forced to surrender 'Northumbria', and from 1164, after the death of William of Mortain and the remarriage of his widow, the honour reverted once again to the crown. Through his sheriffs Henry II gave the county administrative unity. In 1168 the area we once knew as Lancashire was officially described as *the county of Lancaster*, and that which we call Lonsdale north of the Sands was later referred to as *Furness wapentake* and even *Dalton wapentake*.

On his accession in 1189, Richard I granted the honour of Lancaster and other lands to his brother, John, count of Mortain. John interested himself in Lancashire in several ways. He reaffirmed the privileges of the boroughs of Lancaster and Preston and granted a charter to the infant borough of Liverpool. He sold or leased parts of the royal estates to his followers, and, for a price, gave to Lancashire freeholders the right of assart in the royal forests. When he revolted against Richard's government in 1194 the heads of several Lancashire families, including Montbegon, Lathom, Molyneux and Boteler, supported him. But the revolt was unsuccessful, and these Lancashire rebels were fortunate to escape with nothing more than fines totalling £700. They found little to compensate them when John succeeded to the throne in 1199. The strengthening of the royal castles at Lancaster and West Derby brought them little comfort, and though John was ready enough to confirm the privileges he had granted earlier, he demanded new fees and fines. Lancashire families soon began to feel the burden of steady taxation and heavy fines for technical offences. Many of them were very ready to join the general protest of the baronage, and John de Lacy of Clitheroe and Roger de Montbegon of Hornby were among the baronial leaders who forced John to accept *Magna Carta.*

During the minority and troubled reign of Henry III the honour of Lancaster was administered by a sheriff in the name of the crown. There was considerable intrigue and quarrelling over this important office. John's last sheriff, the earl of Chester, strongly opposed Hubert de Burgh, regent for Henry III, and in consequence he was deprived of the shrievalty, which passed to the Ferrers family, the head of which was William, earl of Derby. In 1265, however, young Robert de Ferrers supported Simon de Montfort's rebellion, and at the restoration of Henry III in the following year suffered the forfeiture of his offices and estates. Edmund, Henry III's youngest son, became the new lord of Lancaster.

7. Domesday Book's description of South East Lancashire.

Translation

In Salford Hundred

King Edward [the Confessor] held Salford. There are 3 hides and 12 carucates of waste land and forest 3 leagues long and the same in width, and there are a number of enclosures and a hawk's eyrie.

King Edward held Radcliffe as 1 manor. There [at Radcliffe] is one hide and another hide belonging to Salford.

The church of St. Mary and the church of St. Michael [at Ashton-under-Lyne] held in Manchester 1 carucate of land quit from all dues except geld. To this manor or hundred belonged 21 berewicks [subsidiary manors] which as many thanes held as the same number of manors. In these there were 11½ hides and 10½ carucates of land. There is woodland there 9½ leagues long and 5 leagues and 1 furlong wide.

Gamel, one of those holding 2 hides in Rochdale, was free of his customs except these six—theft, house-breaking, premeditated assault [forsteal], breach of the king's peace, disobeying the reeve's summons, and renewing an affray after swearing not to. For these offences he paid 40 shillings. Others of these lands were quit from every due except geld, and a few are quit from geld. The whole manor of Salford with the hundred used to pay 37 pounds and 4 shillings. At present there are in demesne in the manor 2 plough teams and 8 serfs and 2 villeins with 1 plough team. This demesne is worth 100 shillings.

Of this land of this manor these knights hold by the gift of Roger of Poiton—Nigel 3 hides and half a carucate of land, Warin 2 carucates of land, and another Warin 1½ carucates, Geoffrey 1 carucate of land, Gamel 2 carucates of land. In these lands there are 3 thanes and 30 villeins and 9 bordars and a priest and 10 serfs. Between all they have 22 plough teams. It is worth 7 pounds.

8. Whalley Abbey. The North East Gateway, built late in the fifteenth century.

Edmund held extensive estates in the Midlands and in Wales as well as the honour of Lancaster, but he chose to make Lancaster his principal residence. Before long he was using *earl of Lancaster* as his customary title, and his independence in his estates was as great as that which had been enjoyed by John during the reign of Richard I. In addition to the ordinary revenues of the honour, Edmund appropriated some of the fines from the assize courts and from the pleas of the forest. He exercised the royal right of purveyance within the boundaries of his own estates, and ironically enough, himself appointed the sheriff, whose duties were to safeguard the interests of the crown against encroachment by the earl. In practice his authority approached that of an earl palatine although he never assumed a title that implied such powers. He was most loyal to his brother, Edward I, and he demanded from Lancashire considerable sums of money to help pay for Edward I's campaigns against Prince Llewelyn in North Wales. In 1276, one of the worst years, he authorised the earl of Warwick to recruit troops in Lancashire, and, to the general dismay, ordered the sheriff to close all Lancashire markets, and commandeer food and goods for the use of the king and his army in Wales. Edward's wars against Scotland were to impose even heavier burdens, but in June 1296 before the first Scottish campaign began, Earl Edmund died, and the honour passed to his eldest son, the notorious Thomas of Lancaster.

Lancaster's Borough Seal (reverse)

Thomas was no more than twenty years of age when he succeeded his father as earl of Lancaster, and immediately he was plunged into the urgent business of raising troops for the Scottish wars. The whole of England was taxed to pay for the campaign, and for each of the years from 1297 to 1301 Lancashire was required to make additional contributions of men and arms. In the first year the county raised three thousand foot soldiers and in both 1299 and 1300 two thousand Lancastrians were forcibly recruited for service in Scotland.

On the accession of Edward II in 1307 Thomas of Lancaster was made steward of England. He much resented the presence of Piers Gaveston at court, and his influence in the counsels of the king. In 1310 he led the lords in forcing Edward II to agree to rule through a council of twenty-eight *ordainers,* of whom Thomas was one, and two years later he was mainly responsible for Gaveston's death. Gaveston's place as favourite was taken by Hugh le Despenser, and Lancaster was no more in the real confidence of the king than he had been when Gaveston was alive. He refused to accompany Edward on the Scottish campaign which ended in the battle of Bannockburn, though the following year, 1315, he took command of the army which tried without much success to minimise the after-effects of the English defeat. In 1316 Scottish troops plundered north-eastern England as

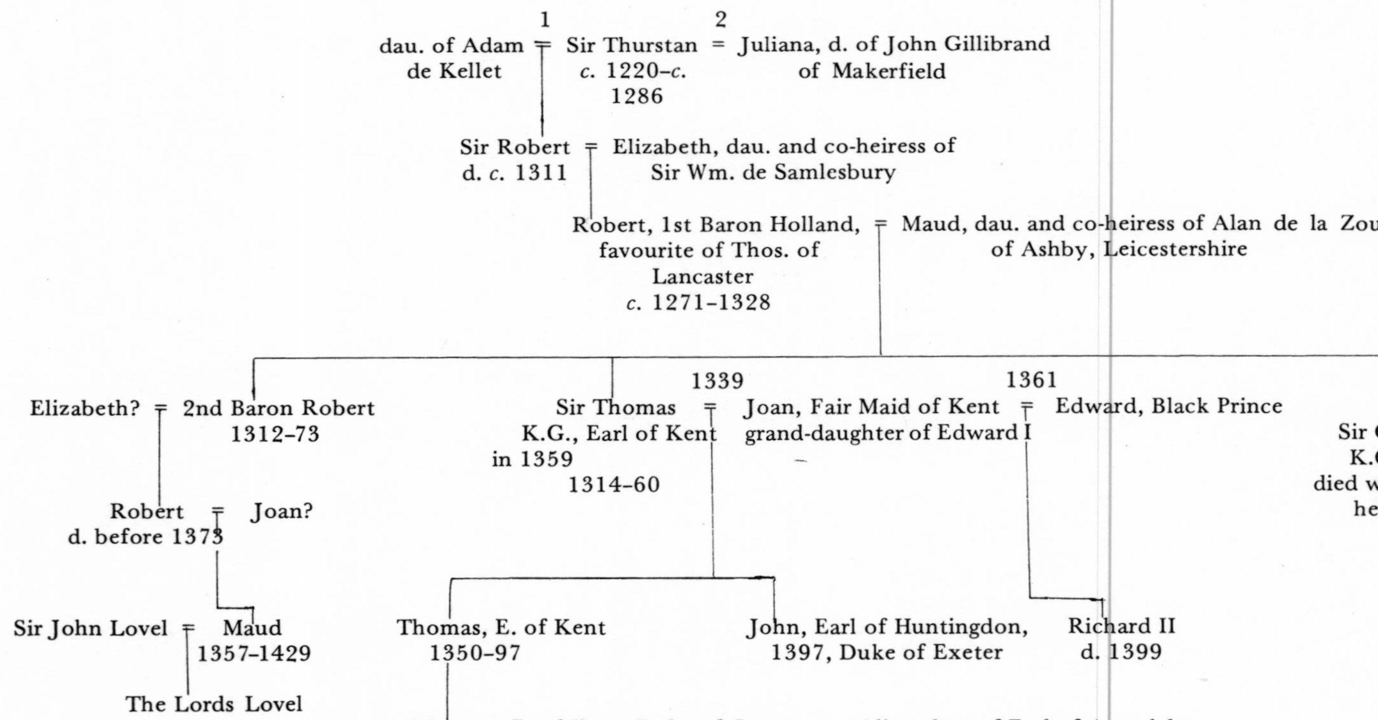
THE HOLLANDS OF UP HOLLAND
1
2
dau. of Adam de Kellet = Sir Thurstan c. 1220–c. 1286 = Juliana, d. of John Gillibrand of Makerfield
Sir Robert d. c. 1311 = Elizabeth, dau. and co-heiress of Sir Wm. de Samlesbury
Robert, 1st Baron Holland, favourite of Thos. of Lancaster c. 1271–1328 = Maud, dau. and co-heiress of Alan de la Zouche of Ashby, Leicestershire
Elizabeth? = 2nd Baron Robert 1312–73
1339
Sir Thomas K.G., Earl of Kent in 1359 1314–60 = Joan, Fair Maid of Kent grand-daughter of Edward I
1361
= Edward, Black Prince
Sir Otto K.G. died without heirs
Robert d. before 1373 = Joan?
Sir John Lovel = Maud 1357–1429
The Lords Lovel
Thomas, E. of Kent 1350–97
John, Earl of Huntingdon, 1397, Duke of Exeter
Richard II d. 1399
Thomas, E. of Kent, Duke of Surrey = Alice, dau. of Earl of Arundel

far as Richmond in Yorkshire and then struck westward to Furness, and in 1322 Robert Bruce himself led a devastating attack along the traditional route into Furness and Cartmel. Near Lancaster he joined the earl of Moray, who had been burning and plundering in Lunesdale, and together the two Scottish forces moved south to destroy Preston. Crowds of panic-stricken refugees fled across the Ribble, and fortunately for south Lancashire the Scots carried their pursuit little further, certainly not beyond Chorley. But hardly a township north of the Ribble had escaped devastation so severe that the effects were felt for a full generation.

Holland Coat of Arms
Azure semée de lis a lion rampant guardant argent

Part of the explanation of the weakness of Lancashire's resistance against the Scots is to be found in the deep divisions which existed between groups of the Lancashire gentry. In 1297 Thomas of Lancaster chose Robert Holland as his most trusted adviser. Holland's grandfather, Sir Thurstan, had considerably advanced the family fortunes by two most profitable marriages, and with the patronage of Thomas of Lancaster, Robert improved the family's position still further. First he was knighted and then raised to the rank of a baron. He was appointed chief justice of Chester, and placed in charge of the castles of Chester, Rhuddlan and Flint. His estates increased rapidly. He castellated his two chief houses at Up Holland in Lancashire and at Baysworth in Leicestershire, and he founded the priory at Up Holland. All these signs of success and the increasing arrogance of Holland himself angered the heads of older Lancashire families, who thought they had more right than Holland to be so favoured by the earl. So long as Edward I's wars against Scotland were being fought and Lancaster was popularly voicing the indignation of the baronage against Gaveston, the Lancashire families stood firmly behind the earl, but in October 1315 Sir Adam Banastre of Shevington and Charnock Richard appealed to his neighbours to overthrow the Hollands. He was rapidly joined by Sir William Bradshaigh of Haigh, Sir Henry Lea of Lea and others, and their joint forces rode south to Wigan and thence to Liverpool. They tried but failed to take Liverpool castle by storm, and therefore retired to Warrington, from where they sent out raiding parties to secure arms from Halton and Clitheroe castles. By the end of October they had moved to Manchester. In the meantime Holland and the sheriff, Sir Edmund Neville, were raising troops, and on 4 November the two armies met in a fierce engagement at Deepdale, just outside Preston. Banastre and his followers were soundly defeated and he, with Lea and several of his supporters, was executed on the field of battle. Others were severely punished by fines and confiscations of land. Sir William Bradshaigh escaped into necessary exile, and his wife, Lady Mabel, believing that he had been killed, married again.

Wigan's Borough Seal

Mab's Cross in Standishgate, Wigan, still stands as a memorial to the penance she made when Sir William returned home again after Lancaster's death.

The uneasy reconciliation between Edward II and Lancaster, which, since the death of Gaveston, had narrowly survived several crises, finally broke down in 1322. At this point, Edward II showed unwonted energy and resolution, and at Boroughbridge defeated Lancaster, Hereford, Clifford and other rebels. The usual punishments followed. Lancaster was executed at Pontefract Castle, and Holland was imprisoned and his estates forfeited. The honour of Lancaster again reverted to the crown, and all those gentlemen in the county who had detested Lancaster, especially Bradshaigh and Thomas Banastre, Sir Adam's heir, sought revenge against Lancaster's favourites. Private warfare, and general opposition to the sheriff's authority added to the horror of the plundering Scottish invasion, and in 1323 Edward personally visited south Lancashire to try and restore law and order. He entered the county through Skipton and Blackburn, held a judicial enquiry at Wigan, stayed for a few days at the newly-built Up Holland Priory, and then visited Liverpool before moving into Cheshire. Any pacification that Edward effected was merely temporary, for there were constant serious riots and defiances of authority in Lancashire, until the major disaster of the Black Death in the years 1349–51 forced gentlefolk and commoners alike to think of other matters for a while. The overthrow of Edward II by Mortimer and Isabella in 1327 led to the release of Holland, but this in turn led to more plots and counter-plots in which both Holland and Bradshaigh were murdered. In 1334 the court of king's bench met in Wigan to try a large number of local offenders, including the sheriff who was accused of extortion and corruption. In 1345 the fair at Lancaster was plundered by bands of armed men, Queen Isabella's treasury at Whalley was robbed of goods worth £3,000, and an irregular force led by Adam Croft from Furness dispersed the King's court at Liverpool and slew a score of men in the presence of the judges. Since 1340 Edward III had been at war with Philip of France, and the new royal demands, which came on top of the steady demands for help against the Scots, made Lancastrians more disgruntled and rebellious than ever.

It is interesting to note that two of Holland's sons, Sir Thomas and Sir Otto, were founder members of the Order of the Garter. In 1339, Thomas, whom Froissart described as 'a great English knight', married Joan of Kent, a granddaughter of Edward I. After Thomas's death in 1360, Joan married the Black Prince, and, therefore, Thomas's two sons, Thomas and John, earls of Kent and Huntingdon respectively, were half-brothers of Richard II. They both played prominent political roles in Richard's reign, and Kent's son was beheaded in 1400 for attempting to overthrow Henry IV. Robert Holland's eldest son, the second baron, had only a granddaughter to succeed him. She married Sir John Lovel, and the Holland estates remained in the Lovel family's possession until a Lovel made the mistake of supporting Lambert Simnel's rebellion in 1487.

Piel Castle or the Piel of Foudray as seen by the Buck brothers in 1727. Lambert Simnel landed on Piel Island, off the Furness coast, in June 1487. He held court in the castle. There he was joined by Sir Thomas Broughton, and from there began the march through Lancashire which ended in defeat at the Battle of Stoke ten days later.

VI The Duchy and County Palatine of Lancashire

Palatinate Seal in William IV's reign (obverse)

Thomas of Lancaster was as ruthless and as perfidious as any of his contemporaries, yet so strong was the reversal of personal and political feeling at the time of the overthrow of Edward II that steps were taken, unsuccessfully be it said, to have Lancaster canonised. In the memory of the nobility he stood out as the most resolute opponent of the hated king. The act of attainder passed against him was reversed, and the earldom and most of his confiscated estates were handed back to his heir, his younger brother, Henry. The rapacious Queen Isabella could not bear to see everything restored, and out of the earldom she retained for life the honour of Clitheroe and the lordships of Rochdale, Penwortham and Tottington. Once Mortimer had been overthrown, Earl Henry achieved his proper place at court as guardian of the person of the young king, Edward III, and first of his councillors. From the beginning Henry exercised on his own estates the same degree of independence which his father, Edmund, had enjoyed. He was hereditary sheriff of Lancashire and controlled completely the local courts, but the more serious crimes were still pleas of the crown, which had to be tried by the king's justices in the assize court at Lancaster. As time went on, however, his privileges, which were redefined and confirmed by a royal charter in 1342, gradually increased. Within the honour all judicial administration was carried out by the earl's officers, and all forfeited lands, possessions and offices passed to the earl and not to the king.

In 1345 Henry of Lancaster died, and his son, another Henry, succeeded to the title as fourth earl. During the first phase of the Hundred Years War the younger Henry had shown himself a most loyal supporter of Edward III and a tireless and successful military commander in Gascony. These services the king rewarded in 1351 by raising Henry to the dignity of duke, a most distinguished honour, for the first English dukedom, that of Cornwall, had been conferred upon the Black Prince only fourteen years earlier. To grace the occasion Edward chose to give Henry, instead of further gifts of land, the privilege of possessing palatinate powers for life. Henceforward Henry was to enjoy the 'liberties and *jura regalia* pertaining to a Count Palatine as fully and freely as the Earl of Chester is known to have them in the county of Chester'. To the head of a county palatine the king transferred most of his royal or 'palace' (Latin–*palatium*) authority in the county. Norman kings had granted wide powers to earls along the Welsh border, and had confirmed the extraordinary jurisdiction of the bishop of Durham, because all these areas needed strong local government capable of repelling border raids and maintaining law and order in difficult circumstances. Lancashire could truly claim that it was a border county against the Scots, although it was not for that reason that it was created a palatinate. To put his new authority into action Henry set up his own chancery or secretariat and appointed his own justices for his own criminal and civil courts. Lancaster and Preston, respectively the seats of the courts and of the chancery, became the Lancashire equivalent of Westminster, for, as the legal phrase had it, no longer did the king's writ run in the county. But in three respects at least palatinate powers in Lancashire were different from those in Cheshire, for Edward III reserved to himself the right to demand parliamentary taxation from Lancashire and to pardon offenders who had been condemned by the duke's judges. Moreover, he still required Lancashire and its four parliamentary boroughs to send representatives to the Commons. Henry's duchy was confined to the boundaries of the county palatine. On his other estates he used one of his subsidiary titles, and therefore in his lifetime Lancashire tended to be referred to as the duchy rather than the county of Lancaster.

Palatinate Seal in William IV's reign (reverse)

Duke Henry died in 1361, and at his death both dukedom and county palatine lapsed. His two daughters, Blanche and Maud, were his co-heiresses. To her husband, John of Gaunt, the fourth son of Edward III, Blanche carried the county of Lancaster, which was her share of the inheritance, but when Maud died unmarried in 1362, the other lands which Duke Henry had possessed also passed through Blanche to Gaunt. Later that year Edward III conferred on his son the title of duke, but declined to give him palatinate powers. Fifteen years later, however, John of Gaunt, with a most favourable parliament behind him, forced the dying king to grant him palatinate powers for life, and in 1390 used Richard II's need of his political support to insist that both duchy and county palatine should be entailed on his heirs male. Gaunt died in February 1399. His son, Henry, had been banished some months earlier, and Richard II therefore seized the duchy lands for the crown. This gave Henry a grievance, which won for him much sympathy when he landed at Ravenspur in June 1399. He successfully challenged Richard II, and gained for himself not only his father's lands and titles, but also the crown of England.

King Henry IV decided to keep all his patrimonial lands separate from the crown lands. With formal parliamentary approval he declared that all estates which he had inherited from his father would

The Gateway, Lancaster Castle. Built c. *1400. Drawn by S. and N. Buck* c. *1725*

henceforward be deemed to be part of the duchy. He established the duchy council, composed of the chief administrative officers of the duchy, to manage the various duchy estates scattered in several parts of the kingdom. The county palatine was now merely the most important part of the duchy, and since the duchy was invested in the king, the continuation of the palatinate carried no threat to the crown. Its longevity was assured. It had its own seal, chancellor, courts and officers; but the duchy council in London, acting in its judicial capacity as the court of duchy chamber, showed its superior position by serving as an appeal court from the chancery court at Preston and by supervising all the judicial work of quarter sessions, as well as doing its main work as a court of equity within the wide boundaries of the duchy. Statute law and common law had as much authority in the courts of the duchy and palatinate as in the king's courts, and this no doubt helped the separate judicial administration of duchy and palatinate to come unscathed through the legal reforms of Henry VIII and William and Mary, and even to recover at the Restoration from the logical blows aimed at it by Barebone's Parliament. It was left to Gladstone's first government to put an end to the palatinate in almost everything but title, for the Judicature Act of 1873 abolished the court of common pleas at Lancaster, took away from the duchy the responsibility for holding assize courts in Lancashire, and placed all civil and criminal jurisdiction in Lancashire under the supervision of the new high court of justice. The act did not abolish the court of chancery, which continued with powers and responsibilities in Lancashire similar to those exercised elsewhere in England and Wales by the chancery division of the high court. Until 1974 it held sessions at three centres, Preston, Liverpool and Manchester. The court of duchy chamber has never met since 1835, and the chancellorship of the duchy has changed from a judicial and administrative appointment to a political appointment.

From 1351 the dukes of Lancaster tried to avoid unnecessary duplication in the administration of duchy, palatinate, and later, kingdom. Thus the first duke gave Henry Haydock, his chancellor, the seals of both duchy and palatinate, and in the fifteenth century this fusion of the two offices became standard practice. It was the deputy chancellor who came to reside in the county palatine. The chancery of Lancaster was deliberately modelled upon the royal chancery, and from the days of Charles II at least, the duchy always chose two justices from among the royal justices on the northern circuit to serve in the civil and criminal courts at Lancaster. When John of Gaunt decided to establish at Lancaster his own exchequer of the palatinate, he used the royal exchequer as the pattern for his own.

9. Rufford Old Hall. The western facade of the timbered Hall built by Thomas Hesketh in the reign of Henry VII. The lantern replaces the louvre which originally allowed the smoke to escape from the fire on the central hearth.

10. Rufford Old Hall. The south-east corner of the great hall. The stone fireplace and chimney replaced the central hearth towards 1600. The origin of the curiously-carved oak screen has caused considerable speculation.

11. Hall-i'-th'-Wood, where, in the 1770s, Samuel Crompton built his spinning mule. The timber-framed wing on the right was built in Tudor times, the stone wing on the left in the 1640s. The whole building was restored by Lord Leverhulme *c*. 1900.

12. Smithills Hall. Part of the fifteenth-century hall is on the extreme left. The gabled building, left-centre, is the family wing of the original H-shaped house. The timber-framed building on the right is Elizabethan in origin.

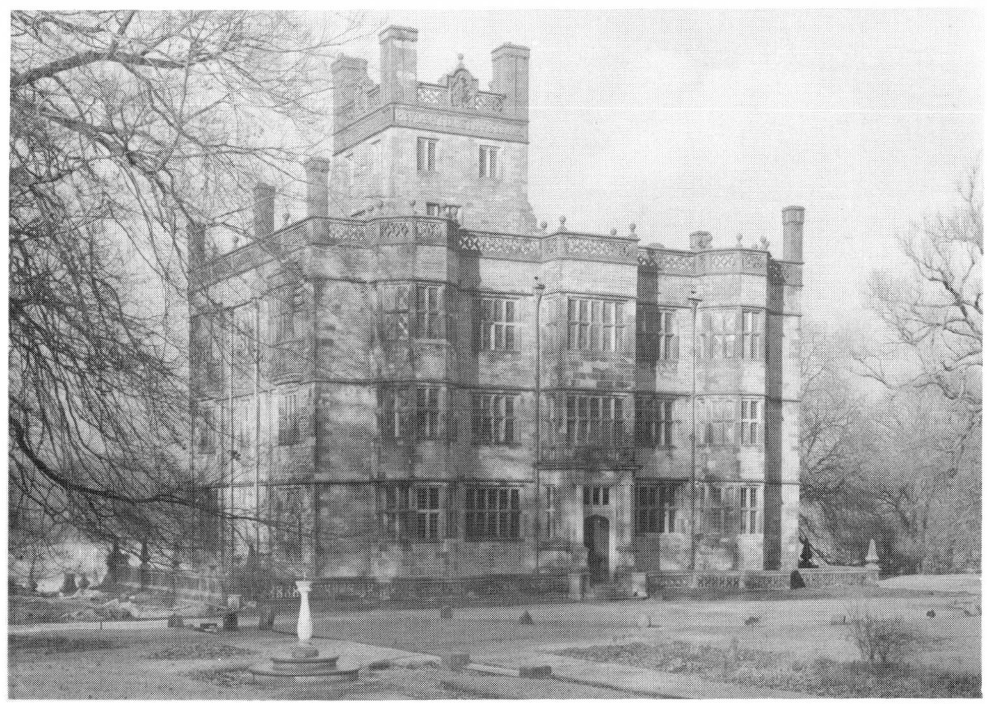

13. Gawthorpe Hall, Burnley. Built 1600-1608 by the Reverend Lawrence Shuttleworth, incorporating a fourteenth-century peel tower. About 1850, James Kay-Shuttleworth engaged Sir Charles Barry, architect of the Houses of Parliament, to modernise the house. Barry's parapet, chimneys and redesigned entrance gave Gawthorpe a more orthodox Elizabethan appearance.

14. Samlesbury Old Hall, between Preston and Blackburn. The oldest parts of the present building date from early Tudor times. The bay window in the centre of the photograph belonged to the original great hall.

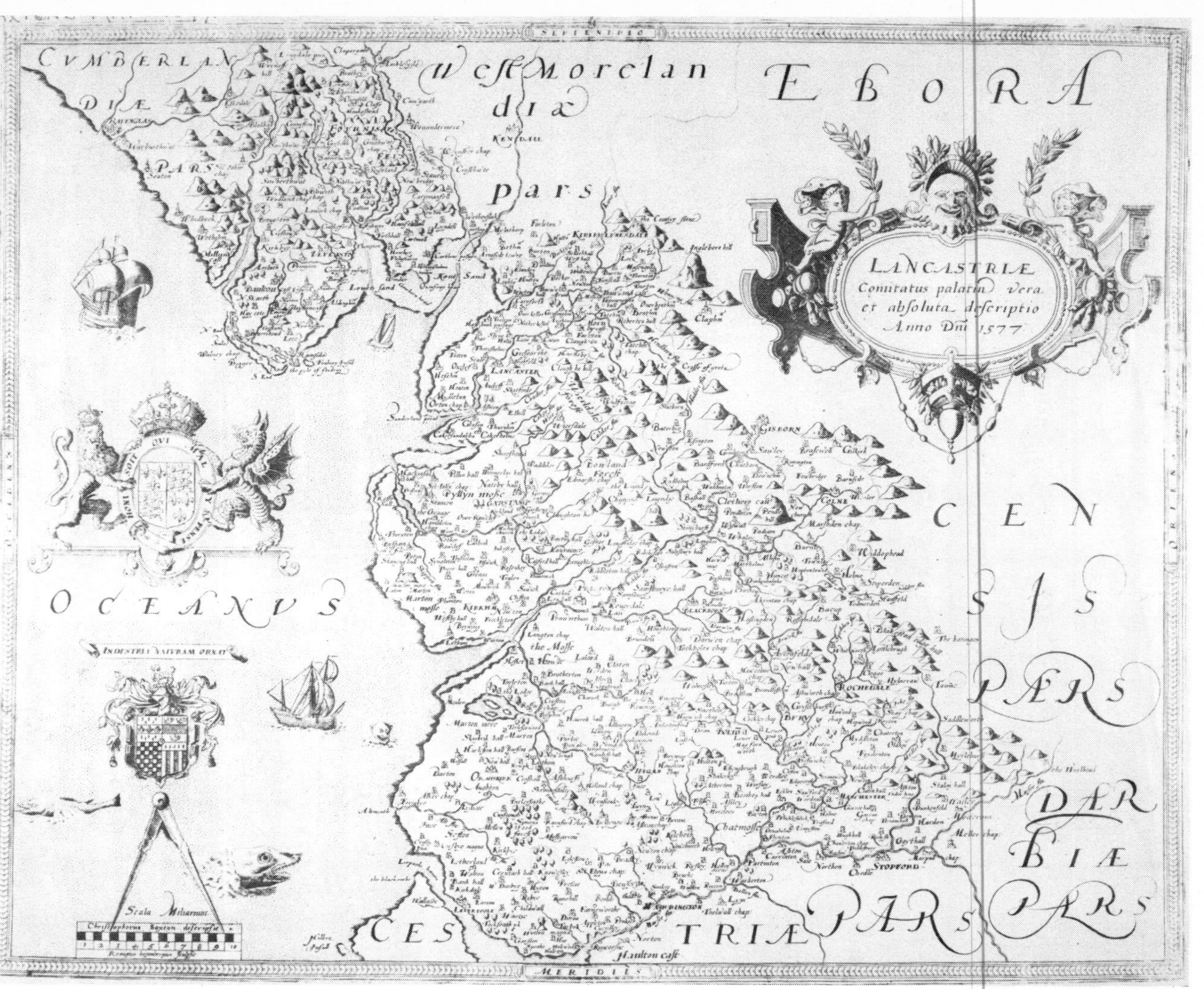

15. Saxtons map of Lancashire, 1577.

He appointed two barons (judges), a chancellor and an auditor, but their work was largely confined to hearing pleas in the exchequer court, because Gaunt still entrusted the collection of rents, fines, taxes and debts to the receiver of the duchy. Late in the fifteenth century the chancery at Preston, at first exercising purely administrative functions, found it necessary to establish a court of its own. This was in accordance with the practice of the time, for jurisdiction by equity rather than by common law had come much into favour. The royal chancery at Westminster was receiving an increasing number of petitions which it settled in its court. It seemed natural that petitions concerning Lancashire should be diverted to the Lancashire chancery court, and by the time Henry VII was duke of Lancaster this court had become a busy one. Like the royal chancery it was bound not by common law, but by equity and by precedents which it gradually compiled.

Arms of John of Gaunt
Quarterly France and England, 3 labels of 3 points ermine

Several lesser offices attached to the duchy and palatinate were in the gift of the crown. For a short period in the sixteenth century the duke appointed a butler to collect dues payable to him for wine brought into the county. Until 1660, when knight's service and feudal tenure *in capite* were abolished, the escheator with his assistants, the feodaries, conducted inquests (inquiries), and particularly *inquisitiones post mortem,* upon lands held by military tenure, and both escheator and feodaries were appointed through the duchy. In the courts at Lancaster and Preston the duke employed the attorney of the county palatine to conduct his prosecutions, just as in the duchy courts he employed his attorney general of the duchy. At Lancaster the duke appointed a lawyer to be the clerk of the pleas of the crown, who was in effect the clerk of the assize court, and another lawyer to be protonotary, or clerk of the court of common pleas. Both these offices came to an end in 1873, although the clerk of the crown merely changed his title to clerk of assize. The clerkship of the peace, or clerkship of quarter sessions, was probably the busiest of these smaller legal offices, because, from Tudor times, so many varied duties were piled on to the shoulders of the justices of the peace and quorum. In Elizabeth's reign the Rigbys of Burgh purchased both this office and the clerkship of the crown. Roger Rigby, clerk of the peace, was not a lawyer and therefore appointed his cousin, Alexander Rigby of Wigan, as his deputy to carry out the duties. Alexander eventually purchased the office himself and it was through his granddaughter, Alice Rigby of Little Hulton, who married Roger Kenyon in 1657, that the office passed into the Kenyon family, where it remained for several generations.

VII *Agriculture and Trade in Medieval Lancashire*

When Adam delved . . .

Domesday Survey shows that in eleventh-century Lancashire there was far more woodland and wasteland than arable land. Salford wapentake had six times as much woodland and nine times as much wasteland as land under the plough; and in West Derby, the most cultivated of all the wapentakes, woodland was almost as extensive as arable land, and mosses or marshes covered five times the area that wood and arable land did together. Five hundred years after *Domesday,* Christopher Saxton, in the first surveyed map of Lancashire, drew a picture of a much more prosperous county. Of the virgin forest only Simonswood, half-scrub and half-moss, remained uncleared. But the mosses were still as extensive as ever. They had defied fumbling medieval attempts to turn their fringes into ploughland, and still lay swampy and treacherous along the Mersey and the Douglas, on both sides of the Ribble estuary, and in the Over-Wyre district of Amounderness.

Lancashire landholders began seriously and continuously to clear the scrub and woodland about the middle of the twelfth century. Periodically they would have their villeins and serfs rooting out the trees and bushes of another *assart* or *ridding,* and in the following summer oats or barley would be growing in the new clearing. But since about a quarter of Lancashire came within the *metes* or boundaries of the royal forest, and therefore under the protection of the severe forest laws, the new *assarts* often involved fines on the landholders. Fortunately they found it profitable to continue the clearing even under the handicap of paying fines, and when John, count of Mortain, became lord of Lancaster, he granted his Lancashire tenants freedom from the forest laws in exchange for the stiff price of five hundred pounds weight of silver. In 1199 John succeeded his brother, Richard I, as king, and for a further two hundred pounds of silver, confirmed the Lancashire privileges. The charter is still preserved in the Lancashire Record Office. It states that King John confirmed, among other lesser grants, the right of the 'knights, thanes and free tenants dwelling in the forests of the Honour of Lancaster' to cultivate their woods at will 'without disturbance of the king's bailiffs'. It was a splendid encouragement well worth the high cost, and during the next two hundred years most of the Lancashire woodlands were cleared.

The mosses, however, remained. Lancashire people took them for granted, but travellers and visitors always remarked upon their extent and their danger. Leland spoke of Chat Moss in a wet season flooding surrounding areas, and in 1698 Celia Fiennes wrote that 'many meres and marshy places' made travel difficult between Wigan and Preston. Mosses had minor advantages in that they yielded turf for burning and, in some places, 'marl' for spreading on the fields, but these were poor compensations for the loss of land and the barrier to communication which they caused. Not until the Industrial Revolution did engineers find a way to drain them, and even then they had to suffer several bitter failures before eventually they succeeded. Today some of the best agricultural land in Lancashire is to be found in those areas which Saxton showed as moss on his map. The springy turf of the footpaths and the deep ditches which drain the black earth are characteristic of these reclaimed lands.

The Anglo-Saxon burh or borough was a strong defensible site. By 1066 about seventy burhs had been established in England, but not one of them appears to have been in Lancashire. Naturally traders and craftsmen sought the protection of the burhs' defended walls, and in time burhs became market towns with certain traditional rights and privileges. The new Norman barons rarely recognised these rights, and the burgesses, usually after a long struggle, had to pay heavy charges if they eventually succeeded in having their independence recognised again. Boroughs situated within the royal domain had to appeal to the crown. Kings Richard, John, Henry III, and Edward I were usually willing to grant borough-charters, but from the end of the thirteenth century charters again became difficult to obtain and even to keep.

In medieval Lancashire four boroughs possessed royal charters. The king usually based a new charter on one already granted to another borough. Thus in 1179 Henry II granted the burgesses of Preston 'all the liberties and free customs of Newcastle under Lyme', and twenty years later King John confirmed the 1193 grant of 'the liberties and privileges of Bristol' to the burgesses of Lancaster. But Preston declares that Henry II's charter was not the first held by the town, and some believe that Roger of Poitou gave Lancaster its first charter in the eleventh century. There is no doubt about Liverpool's beginning. A letters patent, dated 28 August 1207, was addressed to all 'who wish to have burgage-holdings in the township of Liverpul', for King John granted Liverpool both borough and port privileges, in order to build on the banks of the Pool a port convenient for Ireland. In 1246 Henry III granted Wigan a borough charter, which

. . . and Eve span

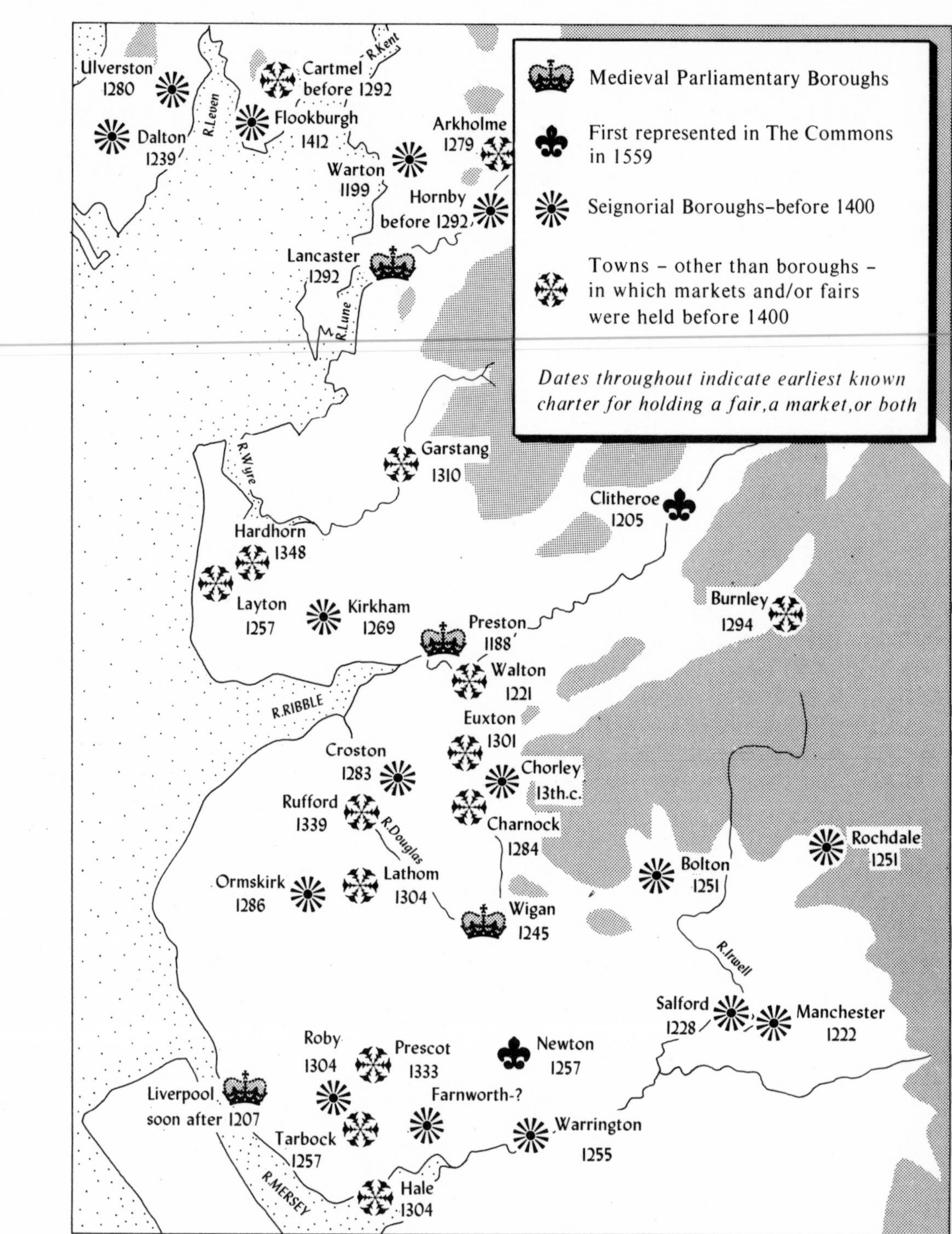

Medieval Boroughs, Markets and Fairs

Preston's Borough Seal

was an extension of trading rights he had conceded the previous year. These four boroughs, administered by mayors and aldermen, had their own courts (courts-leet), and held regular markets and fairs from which they drew considerable fees and rents. A gild merchant, to which all burgesses belonged, regulated the trade and industry of each borough. All four sent 'two worthy burgesses' to the Model Parliament of 1295, but all quickly surrendered this privilege or responsibility because, they pleaded, they could not afford to be represented in the Commons. Liverpool and Wigan sent no members between 1307 and 1547, and Lancaster and Preston no members after 1331 until Henry VIII's Reformation Parliament in 1529.

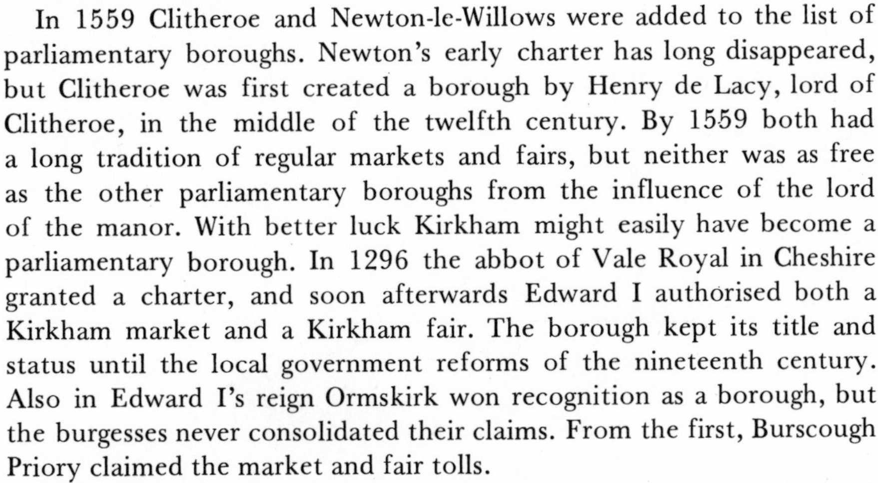

In 1559 Clitheroe and Newton-le-Willows were added to the list of parliamentary boroughs. Newton's early charter has long disappeared, but Clitheroe was first created a borough by Henry de Lacy, lord of Clitheroe, in the middle of the twelfth century. By 1559 both had a long tradition of regular markets and fairs, but neither was as free as the other parliamentary boroughs from the influence of the lord of the manor. With better luck Kirkham might easily have become a parliamentary borough. In 1296 the abbot of Vale Royal in Cheshire granted a charter, and soon afterwards Edward I authorised both a Kirkham market and a Kirkham fair. The borough kept its title and status until the local government reforms of the nineteenth century. Also in Edward I's reign Ormskirk won recognition as a borough, but the burgesses never consolidated their claims. From the first, Burscough Priory claimed the market and fair tolls.

Seigniorial boroughs, which are those granted charters by the local landowner or seigneur, rarely survived many years. Some later lord of the manor usually wished to recover full control of the town, and ordinary burgesses before the sixteenth century had little defence against a determined lord of the manor, however much they had legal right on their side. The burgesses of Warrington fought gallantly but unsuccessfully in the thirteenth century to retain their borough privileges. In 1275 they complained to the king's justices at Lancaster that William Boteler, lord of the manor, refused to recognise their charter rights. The legal dispute lasted until 1292. Boteler won, and the *burgesses* were reduced to the status of *free tenants*. Even Manchester, which by the Tudor period at least was the biggest town in Lancashire, did not succeed in safeguarding its independence. The Grelley family, which owned the manor, had recognised Manchester as a borough in the thirteenth century, but in 1359 a judicial enquiry declared Manchester to be not a borough but a market town. It became a municipal borough only in 1838, six years after the Great Reform Act had granted it representation in Parliament for the first time.

Markets and fairs were held in other places besides boroughs. Both were important institutions, but the fair was the greater occasion. In medieval times, when communications were poor, the arrival of the itinerant merchants provided a welcome contact—unlike invasion—with the world beyond the comparatively isolated communities. It was an event of sufficient moment to bring people from remote hamlets to share in the merrymaking and gaiety and in the more serious business of buying clothes, furnishings and provisions. In short, the fair, which often celebrated a religious festival, served as an important social gathering, and a centre for entertainment, as well as a place for trade. In the main centres, especially on the north-south road, markets were held twice a week. Some of the market days have continued unchanged to the present day.

Medieval Farmers at Work
By courtesy of the British Museum

VIII The Families of Stanley and Molyneux

The Molyneux Arms
Azure, a cross moline or

The stories of the Stanley and Molyneux families illustrate very well the hazards and rewards of land-owning in the Middle Ages. A family's advancement depended upon avoiding minorities, marrying heiresses, and supporting successful groups in political warfare. Its fortunes could be retarded or completely ruined by such accidents as the death of a father early in life, the birth of a daughter instead of a son, or association with an unsuccessful rebellion.

Soon after the Norman Conquest the Molyneux family came into possession of the military fee of Sefton. For several generations the succession worked smoothly. One William Molyneux served with Edward II in the Scottish Wars; a second William fought in France and Spain with Edward III and the Black Prince. But from the end of the fourteenth century the family was dogged by minorities, usually at most important times politically. When Richard II and Henry of Lancaster were disputing the throne, the head of the Molyneux family was a child not yet five years of age, and in 1483, only two years before Henry Tudor overthrew Richard III, Sir Thomas Molyneux died leaving as his heir another young boy. A third long minority occurred in Elizabeth's reign, so that despite distinguished Molyneux service in France under Henry V and again under Edward IV, and despite royal congratulations showered upon William Molyneux for his part in the battle of Flodden—'ye as a verray hertie loving servant acquyted your self . . . to our grete honour and th' advancement of your no little fame and praise'—the Molyneux family did not acquire its first hereditary title until 1611, when Sir Richard was the second person in the whole kingdom to be elevated to the new rank of baronet.

The Stanleys made a far more spectacular rise to fame. They had the good fortune to avoid minorities, to make profitable marriages, and to steer a skilful course through the political rocks of the fifteenth century. They first appeared as a minor landed family on the Staffordshire-Cheshire border in the twelfth century. Over a hundred years later the head of the family was chief forester of Wirral; but the foundations of the family fortune were laid in 1385 when Sir John Stanley, second son of the forester and himself a distinguished soldier, married Isabel, five years later heiress of Sir Thomas Lathom, owner of considerable estates centred upon Lathom and Knowsley in Lancashire. So valuable were the possessions brought into the family

Important Lancashire Families, *c.* 1600

16. Stonyhurst, today a Roman Catholic public school, has been gradually pieced together since 1592-94 when Sir Richard Shireburn built the gatehouse and southern half of the west front. In Anne's reign, Nicholas Shireburn added the cupolas and ponds. The northern half of the west front was only built in the mid-nineteenth century.

Walton Hall, the main residence of the Hoghton family from the early eighteenth century until late Victoria's reign. The Hall was demolished at the beginning of the present century.

18. Dalton Tower, originally a fourteenth-century peel tower, but, with many alterations and additions, has served the town at different times as prison, stable, market hall, local government offices and masonic lodge.

19. Hoghton Tower, *c.* 1800, abandoned by the Hoghton family, and occupied by hand-loom weavers, spinners and calico printers.

Two tourist attractions in the north of the county.

20. (*left*) Leighton Hall, once the home of the Gillow family and still possessing some elegant Gillow furniture.

21. (*below*) The sixteenth-century parish church at Hawkshead, the most northerly town in pre-1974 Lancashire.

22. Johnson's Hillock, Whittle-le-Woods. The Lancaster Canal is on the left: on the right the Leeds-Liverpool Can is beginning its climb over the Pennines by ascending a staircase of seven locks.

by Isabel, that, against all convention, John, the eldest son of the marriage, and his son, Thomas, both gave the Lathom arms preference over the Stanley arms on their shields. Later generations altered this, but kept the eagle and child, the Lathom crest, as their own. In 1405 Sir John, Isabel's husband, was granted the title Lord of Man for remaining loyal to Henry IV during the Percy rebellion. His son and his grandson both increased their possessions by marrying heiresses, so it is not surprising that his grandson, Sir Thomas, was made a baron in 1456. The second baron, another Thomas, married as his second wife Lady Margaret Beaufort, the widowed mother of Henry Tudor, who was destined to become Henry VII of England. Lord Stanley played his political cards most dextrously during Richard III's reign, and earned for his last-minute but decisive support of Henry Tudor at Bosworth the reward of the earldom of Derby. Even more good fortune quickly followed. In 1487 Lambert Simnel crossed from Ireland to Furness, and with considerable Lancashire support made a bid for the throne. He was defeated at the battle of Stoke, near Newark, a battle in which Lord Strange, Derby's son, commanded a large section of the king's army. To Derby Henry gave most of the confiscated estates of Simnel's Lancashire supporters, and the Stanley family succeeded to the Lovel estates in the Wigan area, to the Pilkington estates in Bury, Salford and Manchester, to the Harrington estates both north and south of the Ribble, and to the Broughton estates in Furness and Cartmel. From that moment it was easily the richest and most powerful house in Lancashire.

The Garter Stall Plate of Thomas, 1st Baron Stanley, died 1459

In 1495 Henry VII paid an official visit to his step-father's houses at Knowsley and Lathom. Derby made elaborate preparations to receive the king. He built a new extension to Knowsley Hall, and paid for the reconstruction of Warrington bridge so that the royal party could enter Lancashire without undergoing the ordeal of the ford. King Henry and Queen Elizabeth stayed in Lancashire ten days, and the glittering occasion of their entertainment marked the beginning of an earldom, which was destined to play a major part in most aspects of Lancashire life during the next five centuries.

Charles I created Sir Richard Molyneux, the second baronet, a viscount in 1628, and in 1771 George III bestowed an Irish earldom on the eighth viscount with the title of earl of Sefton. The family made Croxteth Hall its main seat. William, the second earl, nicknamed Lord Dashalong, helped the radicals in Liverpool during the stormy political days which followed the Napoleonic Wars. He was made a baron of the United Kingdom, and is remembered as patron of the first Grand National run at Aintree in 1836.

IX Old-established Lancashire Grammar Schools

Effigy of Lady Margaret Beaufort, 1st Countess of Derby, an enthusiastic patron of the New Learning

During the Middle Ages the Church was the guardian of learning. Abbeys and priories educated their novices, and sometimes, as at Furness, organised a school for boys who lived in the neighbourhood. Secular priests combined the duties of priest and schoolmaster in chantry schools, which were usually endowed by some local landowner for the double purpose of saying special masses for the repose of his soul, and of opening a school in his town or village. These schools were always small, for few parents considered that ability to read and write was necessary unless their son intended to prepare for a profession. Hardly any records of these schools have survived. Schoolmasters were certainly at work in Lancaster and Preston from the thirteenth century, and in Middleton and Manchester from the first half of the fifteenth century, and it may well have been that other schools too existed in medieval Lancashire.

Towards the end of the fifteenth century England began to feel the influence of the new enthusiasm for classical learning, which was spreading across Europe from Italy. Scholars such as Grocyn, Colet and Linacre, the last of whom enjoyed the stipend if not the duties of the rectorship of Wigan from 1519 to 1524, returned from Italian universities inspired by what they had seen of the Italian Renaissance and determined to teach 'the new learning'. In turn they fired others, and laymen as well as clerics endowed new schools or revived old ones. In 1520 Sir Thomas Boteler bequeathed land to the annual value of £10 'to found a fre gramer scole in Werington to endure for ever'. Four years later William Haigh of Wigan left land worth 33s. 4d. towards the maintenance of a school master to teach grammar in Bolton, and Sir Henry Farington made provision for the establishment of 'one fre gramer skoyle' in the church at Leyland. In the following year Hugh Oldham, bishop of Exeter, re-endowed the school at Manchester, just as William Smith, a Lancashire-born bishop of Lincoln, and John Crosse, a Lancashire-born rector of a London church, had earlier endowed schools in Farnworth (Widnes) and in Liverpool. The religious changes and uncertainties, which followed the dissolution of the monasteries in 1536-9 and the dissolution of the chantries in 1546, curtailed such activities. Only at Penwortham (now Hutton Grammar School) and at Clitheroe were new schools founded in Lancashire during the reigns of Edward VI and Mary.

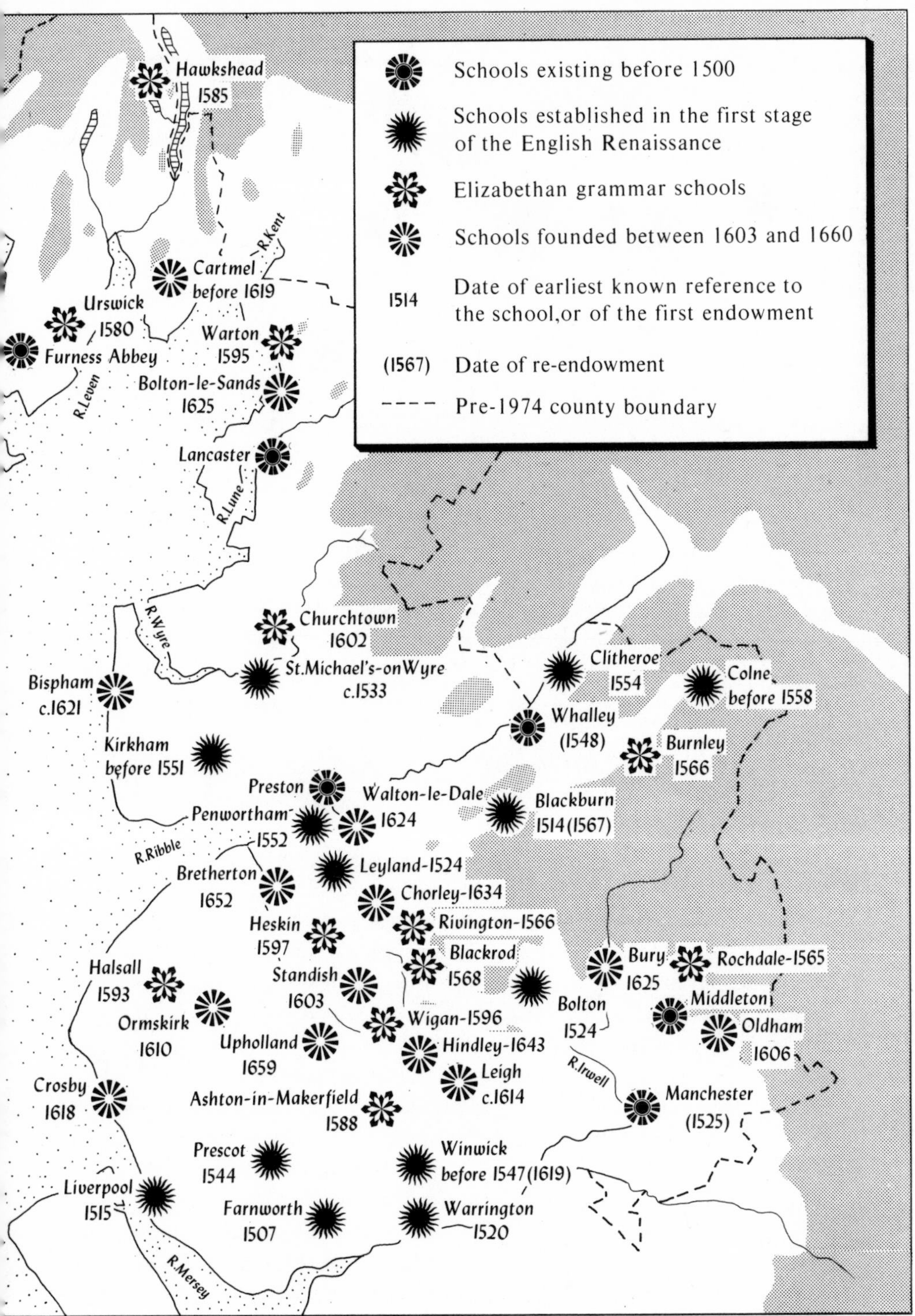

Old-Established Lancashire Grammar Schools

It is a common experience to find evidence of the teaching of Latin in a centre years before the accepted date of the school's foundation. Thus, for example, Hutton's beginning can be traced back to 1517, and Wigan's to the mid-sixteenth century.

Winwick Parish Church. Winwick Grammar School had a high reputation in the seventeenth century

Within a few years of the accession of Elizabeth it was clear that the new Church of England was firmly established, and this prospect of stability, coupled with the steadily increasing prosperity of the middle classes, encouraged gentlemen to endow more schools. Many of these Elizabethan schools are associated with the name of a most distinguished founder, a bishop, an archbishop or even the queen herself, but their founding really derived from local pride and from a middle-class belief in the value of and the necessity for more education. Despite the fact that all these new schools were closely tied to the Church of England, Catholic gentlemen sometimes played a prominent part in their foundation. Sir Thomas Gerard gave the land at Seneley Green upon which Ashton School was built, and Wigan Grammar School was so grateful for the endowment given by another Catholic, James Leigh of Ackhurst Hall, that it embodied part of the Leigh arms in its own coat of arms. The death of Elizabeth did not curtail this educational enthusiasm. Indeed in England there were more grammar school foundations in the reigns of James I and Charles I than there had been under Elizabeth.

These Tudor and Stuart schools were called *grammar* schools because their curriculum was based upon the study of Latin grammar. When a boy entered the Lower School at seven or eight years of age he was set to learn the fundamental rules of Latin grammar, and by the time he moved into the Upper School three or four years later, he had a better knowledge of the language than most Fifth Formers have today. But he knew nothing of mathematics or science, or of a modern language, or of literature or history except that associated with the Romans. In the Upper School he read Latin texts, and, if he stayed at school long enough, he learned to read Greek. All pupils received weekly tuition in the doctrines of the prayer book. The local vicar or curate kept a close eye on the teaching in the school, the scholars regularly attended church services as a school group, and every schoolmaster had to be licensed by the bishop. The more important saints' days, or red-letter days, were observed as holidays, but other holidays were short. A fortnight or three weeks at Christmas was usually the biggest break in the school year. The school day began either at six or seven o'clock for most of the year, and at eight o'clock during the dark days from November to February. Afternoon school ended at four, five or even six o'clock according to the time of the year. The monotony of the curriculum during these long days was made worse by the unchanging method of teaching and the absence of games or physical exercise. Tudor and Stuart schoolmasters saw no virtue in recreations.

X *Catholics and Puritans in Lancashire*

The Elizabethan Church Settlement was designed to offend as few people as possible, but Elizabeth's decision to assume the title of 'Supreme Governor of this realm . . . as well in all spiritual or ecclesiastical things or causes as temporal' could not help but estrange the Roman Catholics; and her decision to rule her church through bishops and to instruct her clergy to wear vestments and to follow the rubrics of the prayer book gravely displeased many Puritans.

Cardinal William Allen 1532-94

Lancashire was the strongest Catholic county in England. From 1567 onwards, especially in Ribblesdale, the Fylde and the south-west, many landed gentry refused to attend their parish church. They were called *recusants,* the refusers to go to church. They encouraged their tenants to follow their example. At first the fine was only 12 pence for each offence, and even this was rarely levied in Lancashire for most of the justices of the peace were either Catholics or Catholic sympathisers themselves. The offence became more serious after Pope Pius V in 1570 had excommunicated Elizabeth, and still more so when ten years later Parsons and Campion came secretly across the Channel to lead a Jesuit mission to win back England to the Catholic faith. Naturally Elizabeth's government henceforward regarded every Catholic as a potential traitor and more severe recusancy laws were passed to try and destroy the Roman Catholic Church in England. From 1581 it was high treason for a priest to say the Mass. Recusancy fines were fixed at £20 a month for non-attendance at the parish church services, and a Catholic landowner could lose two-thirds of his land if he persisted in defying the law. Most Lancashire Catholics endured these penalties with remarkable patience. They took no part in plots against Elizabeth, but they were quietly determined to continue in their faith. In this they were greatly encouraged by such priests as Laurence Vaux, the Blackrod boy who became warden of Manchester Collegiate Church in 1558, and William Allen, a future cardinal who was born at Rossall, and who in 1568 founded the English College at Douai. By secret routes Lancashire Catholics sent their sons to Douai, St. Omer, Rome, and elsewhere in Europe to be educated as priests, and from about 1575 the first trickle of Lancashire-born priests began to return to England. In 1585 Elizabeth's government considered that despite several arrests there were still over a score

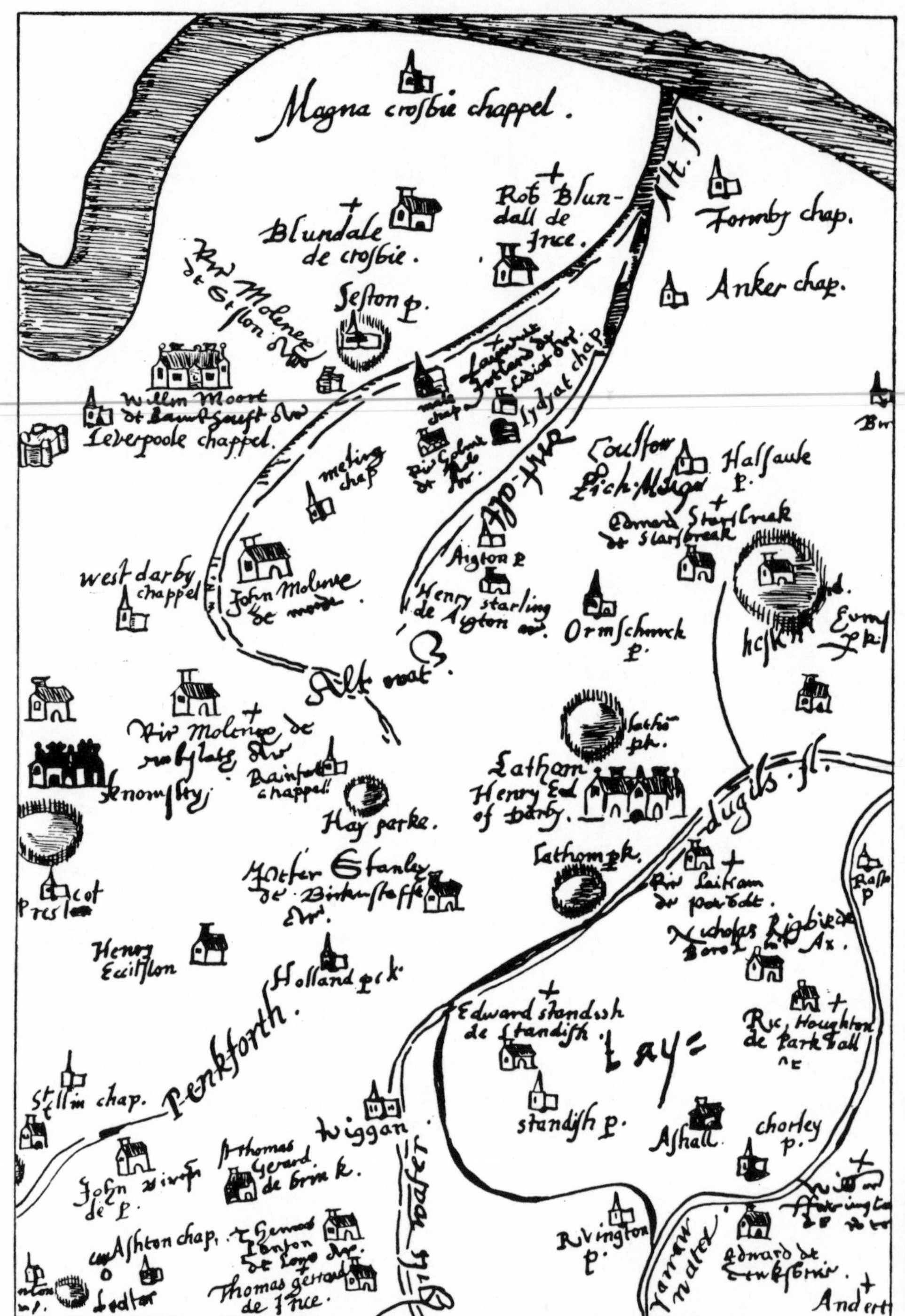

Part of Lord Burghley's Map of Lancashire (redrawn and simplified)

About 1590, Lord Burghley had a map of Lancashire drawn so that, by seeing the relative position of gentlemen's houses, he could more easily take precautionary measures against Roman Catholics. He marked the homes of well-known recusants with a cross. The map is drawn with the west at the top, and this section shows part of the coast between the Ribble and the Mersey.

The original map is in the British Museum, but it has been published by the Catholic Record Society under the title *Lord Burghley's Map of Lancashire.*

of priests secretly active in Lancashire, and in 1581, Campion himself stayed with the Southworths at Samlesbury, the Hoghtons at Hoghton Tower and the Hesketh's at Aughton. The war with Spain increased anxiety, for the government feared a Spanish landing on the Lancashire coast. In 1590 seven hundred Lancashire recusants were brought before the justices and 'yet the number doubted to be far greater'. Some were imprisoned, others fined, but these punishments did not reduce the number of Catholics in Lancashire. In 1641 Pym declared in the Commons that there were 1,800 Lancashire recusants, but official figures in 1667 gave 5,496 for Lancashire, 1,855 for Yorkshire, 96 for Essex, and only 52 for London and Middlesex.

Dean Alexander Nowell, 1507-1602

Manchester and Bolton were the twin centres of Lancashire Puritanism. Without doubt they were encouraged and influenced in their beliefs by the strong connection between the textile merchants of south-east Lancashire and Puritan London, for Puritan merchants ensured Puritan spinners and weavers just as surely as Catholic landowners ensured Catholic peasants. Two of the fellows of the Collegiate Church of Manchester, Alexander Nowell of Middleton, who became dean of St. Pauls, and William Bourne, who worked all his life in the Manchester area, had particularly strong influences. From about 1590 most of the clergy in south-east Lancashire dispensed with surplices. The congregation received the bread and wine at the Communion service either sitting or standing, and, as in London, Lancashire Puritans observed the whole of Sunday as a day of prayer and praise. In 1588 Lord Derby seized and destroyed in Manchester one of the presses that were printing the fanatical Puritan pamphlets known as the Marprelate Tracts. Later, in Charles I's reign, the authorities had far more trouble stopping the secret press at Birchley Hall, near St. Helens, printing Roman Catholic books and pamphlets.

During Elizabeth's reign most Puritans formed a radical group inside the Anglican church, but once James I had declared that he was not in sympathy with Puritan beliefs, a steadily increasing company broke away and formed non-conformist groups. In south-east Lancashire most non-conformists were Presbyterians. Parliament's victory in the first Civil War enabled the Presbyterians to gain control of all religious worship in the county. They divided Lancashire into nine administrative divisions called *classes*, and to each *classis* gave authority to license all preachers and to ordain all clergymen. But the Presbyterians were just as intolerant as any other seventeenth-century church. They opposed the Independents (Congregationalists), Quakers, and other Puritan sects as strongly as they did Anglicans and Roman Catholics. Indeed they welcomed Charles II back in 1660 because they saw no other way of restoring 'necessary discipline' in the religious life of the county. They paid a heavy price for this 'discipline', for when Parliament reimposed the Anglican prayer book in 1662, sixty-seven Lancashire clergy, nearly all Presbyterians, could not conscientiously accept it. They were 'ejected' from their churches. Few of them were as fortunate as Henry Newcome of Manchester who lived to see his church restored by the Toleration Act of 1689.

The Friends' Meeting House, Hardshaw, St. Helens. This building, still used as a meeting house today, was the Quaker centre for south-west Lancashire before and after 1700. From 1652, when George Fox first visited Swarthmoor Hall, Ulverston, Quakerism recruited many devoted followers especially in the north of the county.

XI The Civil War in Lancashire

In Lancashire almost everybody's sympathy in the Civil War was determined by his religious belief. The Puritan-dominated south-east supported Parliament; the Catholic and Anglican north and south-west the king. But no area was solid in its support. Salford was mainly royalist and Liverpool almost wholly parliamentarian, and in most towns and villages there were men whose sympathies were not those of their neighbours. The map shows that, measured by area, the greater part of Lancashire stood for Charles I, but because the population was scattered in the north and parts of the west, measured by numbers, at least as many Lancastrians supported Parliament as supported Charles. The Lancashire representation in the Long Parliament, eight Parliamentarians and six Royalists, probably reflected in due proportion the division of opinion in the county.

Hornby Castle besieged by Parliamentary forces June 1643

Fighting in Lancashire began in September 1642. Lord Strange, soon to succeed his father as earl of Derby, led three thousand Royalists from Warrington to besiege Manchester. The citizens, under the direction of Colonel John Rosworm, a German who had been a soldier in the Netherlands, defended the approaches to the town with mud walls and wooden posts chained together to break up cavalry charges. After a week of unsuccessful attacks Strange withdrew. Weeks of intensive preparation followed, until in February 1643 a struggle began for the control of the main north-south road. Lancaster, Wigan, Preston and Warrington were held first by one side and then by the other in attack and counter-attack, but by June the Parliamentarians, under the command of Ralph Assheton of Middleton, firmly occupied these four key towns. Indeed before the end of 1643 the Royalists held only Lathom House near Ormskirk and Greenhalgh Castle near Garstang. Then, in February 1644 Colonel Alexander Rigby laid siege to Lathom House, which was defended by the countess of Derby with three hundred troops. But the Parliamentarians' lively hope of complete victory was dashed when Prince Rupert led strong forces through Cheshire, swept aside opposition at Stockport, savagely attacked Bolton, re-occupied Wigan, plundered Liverpool after a fortnight's siege, and freed Lathom House. From these triumphs Rupert crossed into Yorkshire only to meet defeat at the hands of Fairfax, Cromwell and the Scots at Marston Moor on 2 July. A fortnight later Rupert and his surviving Royalist followers, who had so

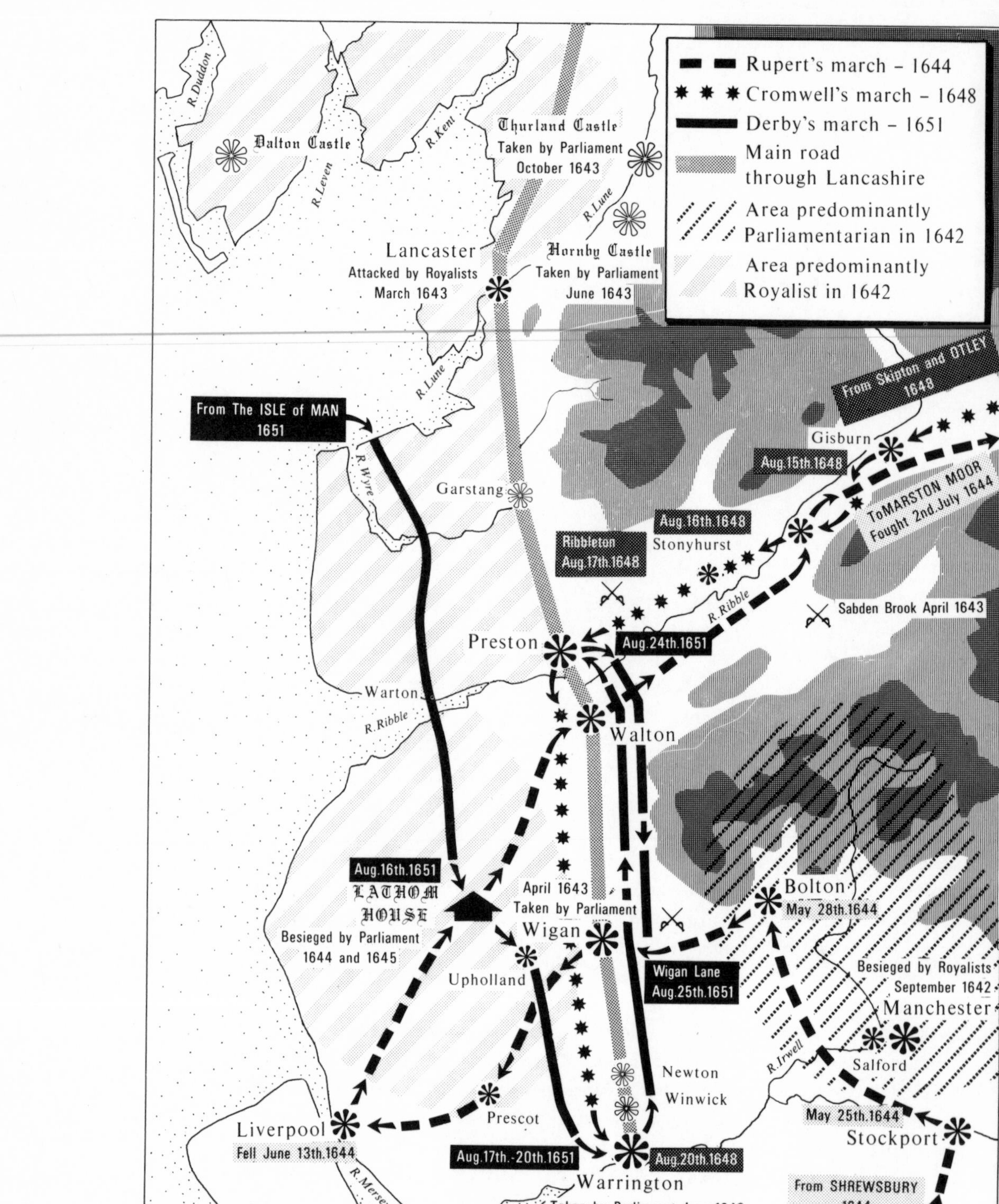
Rupert's march - 1644
Cromwell's march - 1648
Derby's march - 1651
Main road through Lancashire
Area predominantly Parliamentarian in 1642
Area predominantly Royalist in 1642
R.Duddon
Dalton Castle
R.Leven
R.Kent
Thurland Castle
Taken by Parliament
October 1643
R.Lune
Lancaster
Attacked by Royalists
March 1643
Hornby Castle
Taken by Parliament
June 1643
From Skipton and OTLEY
1648
From The ISLE of MAN
1651
R.Wyre
Gisburn
Aug.15th.1648
Garstang
ToMARSTON MOOR
Fought 2nd.July 1644
Aug.16th.1648
Ribbleton
Aug.17th.1648
Stonyhurst
R.Ribble
Sabden Brook April 1643
Preston
Aug.24th.1651
Warton
Walton
Aug.16th.1651
LATHOM HOUSE
Besieged by Parliament
1644 and 1645
April 1643
Taken by Parliament
Wigan
Bolton
May 28th.1644
Upholland
Wigan Lane
Aug.25th.1651
Besieged by Royalists
September 1642
Manchester
Salford
R.Irwell
Newton
Winwick
Prescot
Liverpool
Fell June 13th.1644
May 25th.1644
Stockport
Aug.17th.-20th.1651
Aug.20th.1648
Warrington
Taken by Parliament June 1643
R.Mersey
From SHREWSBURY
1644

Civil Wars, 1642-1651

recently left Lancashire in high spirits, were back in the county, hastening home. The Parliamentarians soon recovered all they had temporarily lost. Lathom House was besieged again, but the garrison defied the Parliamentarians until December 1645, by which time the first civil war was virtually over.

Eighteenth-century representation of the execution of James, earl of Derby, 1651

The Second Civil War began in 1648. The Scots supported Charles on the understanding that Presbyterianism should be the official religion in England for at least three years. The Lancashire Presbyterians, however, continued their support of Parliament, and many of them marched with Assheton into Westmorland to oppose Hamilton's Scottish army. Hamilton commanded about twenty-four thousand men, a very formidable force, but foolishly he allowed them to straggle. At times more than twenty miles separated the leading forces from the rearguard. On 13 August, Cromwell, who had wrongly anticipated that the Scots would march through Yorkshire, decided to strike from Otley at the Scottish flank by marching quickly down the Ribble valley. His speed and his tactics completely defeated the leisurely Scots. A skirmish at Ribbleton gave him control of Preston and the bridge at Walton, and then in a running battle along the road to Warrington he put the Scots to flight. Four thousand were taken prisoner near Warrington bridge. Hamilton himself surrendered in Shropshire.

This battle of Preston sealed the fate of Charles I, but in 1651 the Scots invaded north-west England in the name of Charles II. Derby, who was still holding the Isle of Man for the king, decided to help them. He landed a small force at the mouth of the Wyre, crossed the Ribble and began to recruit in the south-west. But the fifteen hundred men he gathered together were untrained, and on 25 August they were defeated by Colonel Lambert's regiments at the battle of Wigan Lane. Sir Thomas Tyldesley, the best soldier among the Lancashire Royalists, was killed, and Derby himself, after he had fought for Charles II at Worcester, was taken prisoner a few days after the battle by a Lancashire captain, Oliver Edge. He was tried at Chester and condemned to die at Bolton. Derby appealed against this assumption that he was responsible for the indiscriminate slaughter at Bolton in May 1644. He wrote to William Lenthall, speaker of the House of Commons, that he had cleared himself of such a charge 'by undeniable evidence', but the decision was not changed. When on 16 October 1651 the axe fell, it ended the life of the most devoted supporter of the Stuarts and signalled the close of a distressing chapter of Lancashire history.

In the month following her husband's execution the countess of Derby was forced to surrender the Isle of Man and, though her life was spared, she was kept a prisoner in Rushen Castle until the Restoration.

XII Lancashire and the Jacobites

John Byrom, who witnessed the Jacobite occupation of Manchester in 1745

The Lancashire Catholics were naturally disappointed that hopes roused by James II's accession were so quickly crushed by the Revolution of 1688, and the accession of William III. Just as naturally the new Whig government suspected that the Lancashire coast was a likely place for the Jacobites, the supporters of James II, to stage a rebellion. It was close to Ireland and Catholic support could be relied upon. Certainly there were many suspicious comings and goings. In June 1689, Threlfall, a Catholic from Goosnaugh, and an unknown Lunt landed at Cockerham, and began to deliver to Catholic gentlemen on both sides of the Pennines military instructions and commissions signed by James II. In the following February an Irishman named Kelly informed the magistrates at Evesham in Worcestershire that he had knowledge of a Jacobite plot in Lancashire, and he even named a number of gentlemen, including Molyneux, Towneley and Blundell of Ince, who, he said, were preparing for revolt. This evidence was supported by statements made elsewhere by two other informers, as well as by the disturbing fact that many Irishmen were being employed on west Lancashire farms. But the battle of the Boyne in July 1690 and the defeat of the French fleet at La Hogue in 1692 disrupted Jacobite plans for retaking control of England. Suspicion of treason in Lancashire died down until the summer of 1694, when Lunt voluntarily made a full confession of his activities. The most startling result was the Manchester treason trial. The eight accused were Viscount Molyneux of Sefton, Sir William Gerard of Bryn, Sir Rowland Stanley, father-in-law of Robert Blundell of Ince, Sir Thomas Clifton of Clifton in the Fylde, William Dicconson of Wrightington, Philip Langton of Hindley, Bartholomew Walmsley of Blackburn and William Blundell of Little Crosby. They were all in grave peril, because persons accused of treason were given little chance to defend themselves, and death was the only possible penalty. Yet all were found not guilty, and at the next Lancaster assizes they successfully prosecuted for perjury the three chief witnesses against them. It was a most sensational affair. In the Commons the government had to justify the prosecution, and in the following year the law concerning treason trials was amended. The government could hardly be blamed for taking action. There had been so much Jacobite smoke in Lancashire that it was logical to suspect that Jacobite fire was there too.

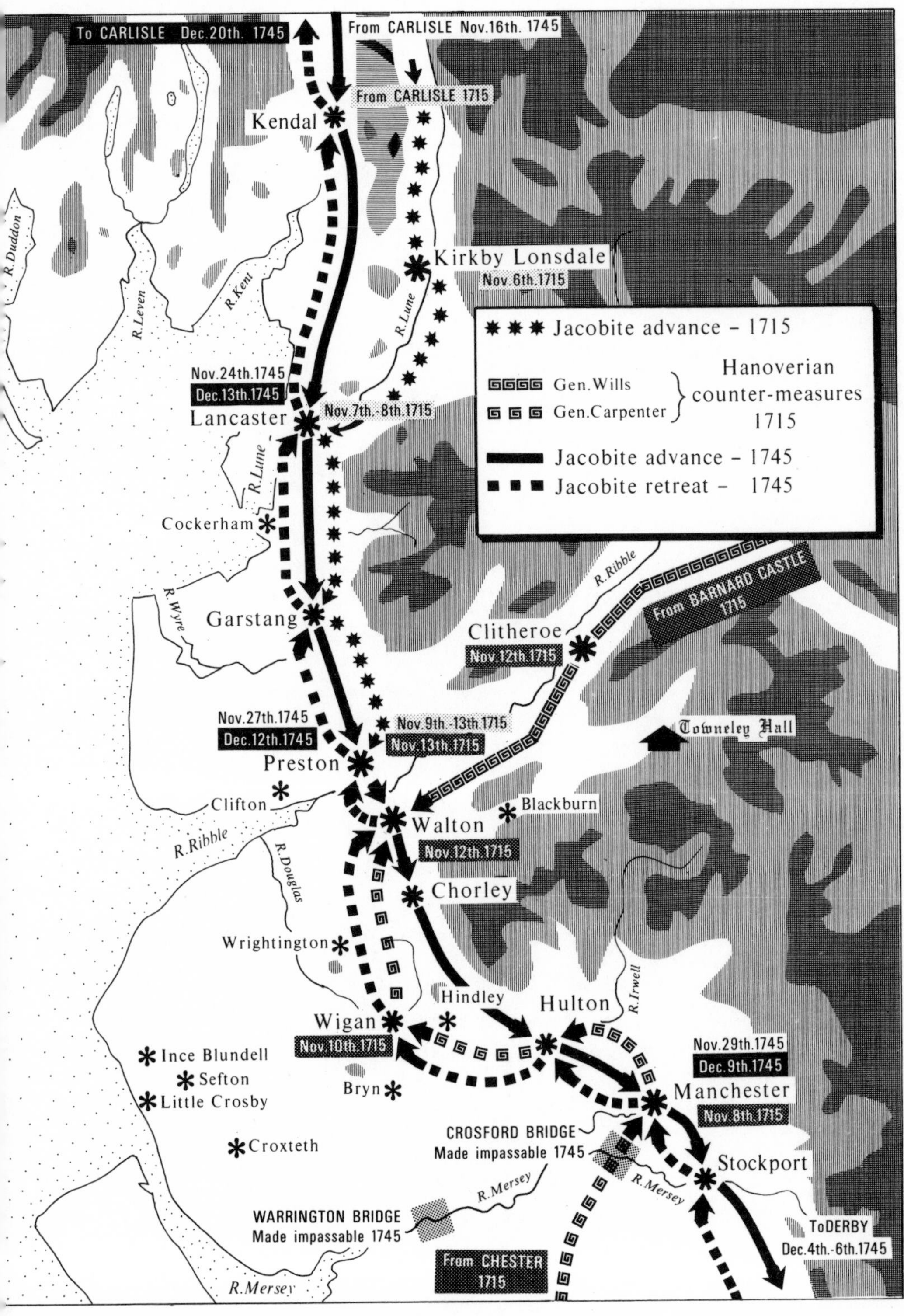

Jacobites, 1715 and 1745

Towneley Hall, Burnley, in the eighteenth century

Queen Anne succeeded William III, and on her death in 1714 the crown passed to George, elector of Hanover. The Jacobites considered that the claim of James Edward, James II's son, should be acknowledged, and in June 1715 at both Warrington and Manchester noisy and violent demonstrations were made in his favour. Thomas Sydall, a Manchester blacksmith, led attacks on the Presbyterian chapel in Cross Street and on other dissenters' chapels in south-east Lancashire. In the following September a much more serious attempt to replace George I by 'James III' was made in Scotland. The Lancashire Jacobites invited the Scottish Jacobites to invade England by way of Lancashire. The invitation was accepted, and on 7 November James Edward was proclaimed king at Lancaster. Three days later a force of about four thousand Jacobites had reached Preston, but two government armies were by now fast converging on the town. On Sunday, 13 November, the Jacobites surrendered. Executions were carried out in various centres in Lancashire as a warning against further attempts at revolt, and among those executed was Sydall, the blacksmith.

For thirty years little was heard again of Jacobitism, but in 1745, when England was engaged in war in Europe, Charles Edward, the son of 'James III', landed in the Hebrides. The Scots welcomed Bonnie Prince Charlie. He entered Edinburgh in September, and held his court at Holyrood. He then marched south, and on 24 November arrived at Lancaster at the head of five thousand men. Quickly he moved to Preston, thence to Manchester, where he was joined by Colonel Francis Towneley and two hundred Lancashire Catholics. At Derby Charles wanted his officers to risk all on a march for London, but they, fearing that they were marching into a trap, urged him to retreat before it was too late. Reluctantly he had to agree, and immediately thousands of waverers decided that his was a cause which it was unsafe to support. By 12 December his troops were back in Preston. A week later in Carlisle, Towneley bade Charles farewell, and tried to hold the town against government forces under the duke of Cumberland. He failed, and twenty of his officers and nearly a hundred men were sent to Newgate prison in London. In July 1746, three months after Charles Edward had been finally defeated at Culloden Moor, nine of these prisoners were executed. They included Towneley himself, and Thomas Sydall, the son of the blacksmith.

XIII *The Common Council of the Borough of Liverpool*

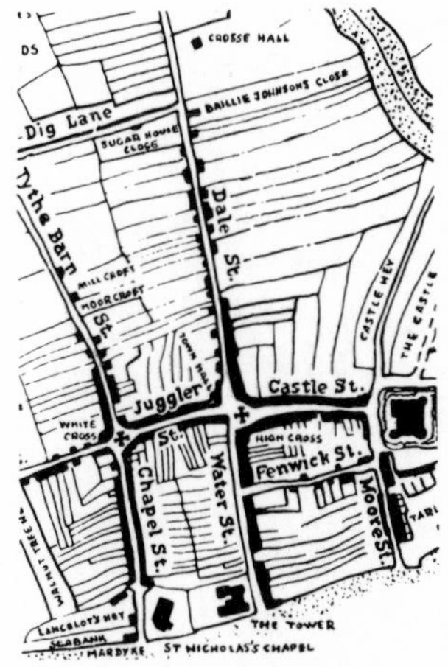

Liverpool, c. *1665*

Authority in Tudor Liverpool lay partly with the assembly of burgesses and partly with the portmoot. The assembly, which had evolved from the medieval gild merchant, elected the freemen who voted in parliamentary elections, and each year on St. Luke's Day, 18 October, appointed a new mayor and one of the two new bailiffs. The mayor chose the second bailiff. A few days later the portmoot, or borough court, voted into office for the coming year a score or more lesser officials, churchwardens, moss reeves, market overseers, rate assessors, etc., as did manor courts and vestries in manors and parishes all over England. The mayor, advised and helped by ex-mayors, *the mayor's brethren,* governed the town through his bailiffs, and all cases of breach of burghal customs were heard in the portmoot by a jury impanelled by the baliffs. It was a democratic but clumsy system, and in 1580 Edward Halsall, the first recorder of Liverpool, induced the burgesses to replace it with the rule of a common council, which would act as legislature and judicature, and supervise the work of the town's executive officers. By James I's reign this close corporation was firmly established, and its dozen aldermen and two dozen councillors were battling strongly for borough rights. They rejected the claim that West Derby copyholders enjoyed traditional rights in Liverpool's 'waste'. They challenged the court of duchy chamber about the jurisdiction it claimed to hold inside the borough, and they strove to establish full control over the town's officials. So insistent was the council on this last point that in 1629 it took away the burghal rights of a bailiff who dared to challenge its ruling in the court of king's bench, and in 1637 it successfully insisted upon dismissing the town clerk, Robert Dobson, despite his appeal to the assize court against the council's judgment. The council long sought a new charter, which would redefine its rights and privileges. It petitioned James I in vain, but in 1626 succeeded in buying one from the recently crowned Charles I. The charter admitted Liverpool's claim to be an incorporated borough, and renewed its authority to hold its own court and make its own bye-laws, but it clearly stated that supreme authority lay not in the common council but in the assembly of burgesses. In the following year, however, the assembly re-elected the council to continue as the governing body in the town.

One of the most difficult legal points to settle in Tudor and Stuart Liverpool was the authority of the lord of the manor. In 1537

Henry VIII had leased the manor rights to Sir William Molyneux of Sefton, and a century later Viscount Molyneux purchased the freehold of the borough for £400 from the city of London, to whom Charles I had sold it in partial settlement of a debt. Naturally the Molyneux family disputed with the council encroachments which it had gradually made upon the manorial rights, in much the same way as in the 1620s John Bridgeman, lord of the manor of Wigan, had contested rights traditionally claimed by Wigan's mayor and aldermen. Within two years Richard, the second Viscount Molyneux, had extracted from the council, 'without prejudice to its rights', an annual payment of £20 for the privilege of having a town mill and a town ferry. But the Molyneux family, strongly Royalist, temporarily lost the lordship of the manor during the Civil War and Interregnum years, and it was not until after 1660 that Caryll, the third viscount, could renew his brother's campaign for full rights. He rejected the council's offer to renew the payment of £20 a year, but in 1668 agreed to terms, by which the council undertook to pay £30 a year for all manorial rights except the ferry and the burgage rents. In his turn, Molyneux, constable of Liverpool castle as well as lord of the manor, recognised the council's rights to control and develop the waste by paying the council two pence a year for the privilege of building a bridge across the Pool at the bottom of the new street, Lord Molyneux Street (now Lord Street), which he had driven through the castle grounds and orchards. By Charles II's reign the out-of-date castle was partly demolished, but in James II's reign, Molyneux, a leading Roman Catholic, stored arms there. The council protested, but the castle was outside the liberties of the borough, and not until after Molyneux had been deprived of the constableship in 1694 for suspected Jacobite sympathies was the council able to gain temporary possession. In 1704 the council purchased a fifty-year lease of the site with power to pull down the ruins, and though the Molyneux family struggled to regain control, by 1726 the last of the castle walls had been demolished.

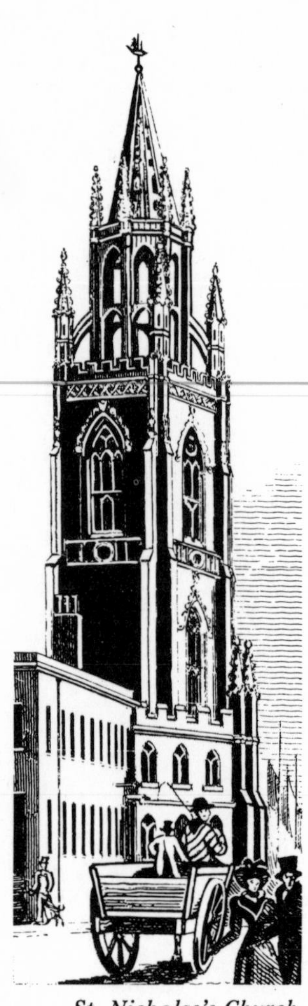

St. Nicholas's Church in the nineteenth century

A quarter of a century earlier, in 1699, Liverpool had ceased to be part of Walton parish. The ancient chapel of St. Nicholas and the new church of St. Peter became the twin centres of the new parish of Liverpool. In 1777, for £2,250, Liverpool bought from Charles Molyneux, first earl of Sefton, the rights of the lordship of the manor. At last the borough could feel to be in full control of its own affairs.

The burgesses of Liverpool retained some authority in the town in that they elected the mayor and bailiffs, and in that the two bailiffs automatically became permanent council members at the end of their year of office. During the Civil Wars most Liverpolitans were staunchly Puritan, and at the Restoration many took exception to the terms of

The Courthouse and Bridgewater Canal, Worsley. The Bridgewater, the second canal in England, was opened in ;1; it was the joint achievement of the Duke of Bridgewater, John Gilbert and James Brindley. The Courthouse is :torian Tudor, built in 1849 by the first Earl of Ellesmere, a descendant of the Duke.

24. The Canal Aqueduct at Barton. (*above*) A barge leaving the steel swing aqueduct, which replaced Brindley's construction when the Irwell was deepened and widened to become part of the new Manchester Ship Canal. (*below*) Brindley's stone aqueduct, lined with puddled clay, which carried the Bridgewater Canal across the Irwell from 1761 to 1894.

25. Crossing Chat Moss 1831. George Stephenson "floated" the line across the Moss on a foundation of brushwood and heather.

26. Tunnel building at Edge Hill.

27. Colne Market Place, early in the nineteenth century: on the left is the Hole in th' Wall Inn, which figures in Robert Neill's *Song of Sunrise.*

28. The Free Trade Hall, Manchester, so named to mark the fight of such local men as Richard Cobden and John Bright against the Corn Laws and other protective tariffs (see pages 103-5). The Hall, rebuilt and modernised after wartime damage, has long served the city as a political forum, and is the traditional home of the Hallé Orchestra which was founded in Manchester in 1858.

the Corporation Act and to the expulsion of Puritan ministers. In 1669 the burgesses elected as mayor one who had refused to take the oath required by the Corporation Act. In reply the 'Cavalier' majority in the council tried but failed to prevent the popular election of bailiffs, and in 1676, the Whig mayor, without consulting the council at all, made matters worse by appointing a substantial number of new freemen just before election day. The council therefore petitioned the king for a fresh constitution, and in the new charter granted in July 1677, Charles II gave the Liverpool Tories all the safeguards they could hope to acquire. Henceforward the council of sixty members was to include fifteen non-resident burgesses, who in practice were Tory landowners living in south-west Lancashire. The council was to elect a mayor, bailiffs and freemen, and when Thomas Johnson and other leading Whig members refused to take the oath required under the new charter, their resignations were assumed and Tories were appointed to the vacancies. After a temporary reconciliation of the parties during the 1688–9 constitutional crisis, the burgesses recovered their rights by voting for Whig M.P.s, who in 1695 successfully petitioned the crown for yet another charter. The Tories, or 'old charter men', fought a rearguard action, but the Whigs maintained their power and popularity in Liverpool for the next fifty years. The 1695 charter lasted until close corporations were swept away by the Municipal Corporations Act of 1835. From then until 1974, Liverpool was divided into wards each of which was represented in the council by one alderman and three popularly-elected councillors.

Blue Coat Hospital, Liverpool, built 1716-18

During the last half century of the life of the close corporation the Tories had the better of the party struggle, but in December 1835, at the first election under the new act, the new householder-voters of Liverpool returned forty-three Whigs against five Tories. Only three members of the old close corporation became members of the new council.

XIV Rich and Poor in Tudor and Stuart Lancashire

Detail of plaster ceiling at Astley Hall, Chorley

On 29 August 1667 at Lancaster assizes, eight prosperous Lancastrians were 'disclaimed' and solemnly charged that they should not 'from henceforth by any ways or means use or take upon them the names of Esquire or Gentleman, unless they be thereunto authorised . . .'. At the same time all 'Sheriffs, Commissioners, Archdeacons, Officials, Scriveners, Clerks, Writers or others whatsoever' were threatened with penalties if they used the title *gentleman* to describe any of those, who that day had been 'reproved, controlled and made infamous of that name and dignity'. Despite the fierce tone of this disclaimer it had little practical effect, for the titles of esquire and gentleman were, in practice, bestowed by common estimation. Distinctions between the different strata of society were real enough, but the strata were no more exclusive than the distinctions were sharply defined. Success in landowning, business, or the clerical and legal professions was widely appreciated, and was likely to win recognition in spite of lowly birth. The grammar schools and the speculative nature of business did most to keep Lancashire society from remaining static in the two centuries before the Industrial Revolution.

In Tudor and Stuart days Lancashire's population was small enough for a gentleman to be acquainted with most other gentlemen in the county. As boys and young men, many had met at Gray's Inn, for from Elizabeth's days, it was increasingly common for landowners to send their sons for a couple of years or longer to the inns of court–and Gray's Inn was the favourite of Lancashire men–in order that they would be better able to carry out their duties as justices, and be armed against the all too common litigious neighbour. Throughout their active lives gentlemen of different areas met periodically at quarter sessions, local fairs, in the hunting field, and at country race-meetings, where young owners rode their own horses and wagered gaily on the result. Even Puritan gentlemen were interested in a good-mouthed hound or a well trained sparrow-hawk, and many who were not Puritans occasionally rode far afield to enjoy cock-fighting, bull-baiting or dog-coursing. Knowledge of farming and skill in riding and the care of horses were necessary parts of a gentleman's education, for though he might be chiefly interested in his business or profession, every gentleman farmed land, and it was as essential to keep three or four horses at least for his own and his family's use, as it was to have cows and pigs in the shippons and sties at the back of the house. Everyone rode horseback, and even when coaches began to churn up Lancashire lanes in the eighteenth century, most gentlemen preferred to ride a horse and leave the coach for their womenfolk and children.

The entrance to Wardley Hall, Worsley

Gentlemen took a pride in their property. Often they would accept the acute embarrassment of being without ready cash in order to spend money on acquiring more land, building a gate-house, modernising or enlarging their fireplaces, or adding extra rooms to their home. They did not hesitate to borrow from relatives and friends, or from those business men who, as a profitable side-line, lent money at six per cent. interest. It was respectable enough both to lend and to borrow, because the seventeenth century recognised that it was often profitable to pay 'use money', in order to have cash available when coveted property was for sale, or when it was inconvenient to convert land or stock into money. Yet despite this competitive spirit in building and improving houses, the homes of most Lancashire gentlemen were very similar in many respects. They were rarely well furnished. Important items such as the dining table or great 'ark' or chest served three or four generations. Floors were mostly uncovered, for the 'carpets' which frequently appear in household inventories were used to cover tables, benches or walls. Linen and silver were prized, but used only on special occasions. In all but the biggest houses pewter-ware, holland sheets and canvas towels were for everyday use. But the kitchen was well-stocked, especially with bacon and salted beef, and the kitchen garden provided the peas, beans, turnips and green vegetables with which to garnish it as long as supplies were available. In the outhouses at the back of the house beer was brewed, and cheese and butter made from the surplus milk, and it would be surprising not to find a row of beehives in the garden. The few essentials the household did not provide were bought at the local market and fair, or from established tradesmen especially in Manchester, Preston and Wigan. Occasional purchases, especially at Christmas-time, were made in London. The carrier delivered, or more generally left for collection in Manchester, the box containing such luxuries as perfumes, spices, toilet soap, cosmetics and more fashionable hats and dresses than could be bought or made locally. His charge for carriage from London was usually no more than a penny or two pence a pound. Labour was cheap, and gentlemen found it easy to maintain a large staff of servants. The more important slept on feather beds up and down the house, and the others on chaff beds in the lofts over the stable or the brewhouse.

At the other end of the social scale, and separated from the esquires and gentlemen by the yeoman farmers, the shop-keepers, the journeymen and the household servants, was a large, miscellaneous group of

Turton Tower, originally a peel tower

unskilled workers. Out of this class came the paupers. Both Tudors and Stuarts were vexed with the problem of the sturdy beggar. Successive Tudor acts of parliament sought the cheapest and most effective means of both discouraging the pauper and keeping him alive, and eventually the acts of 1598 and 1601 established a poor law system, which, with various amendments, lasted until 1929. The Elizabethan Poor Law—the usual name for these two acts—required that paupers who were 'whole and mighty in body' should work for any food and shelter they received. In 1620 the Lancashire justices opened at Preston a county house of correction 'to set rogues, vagabonds or other idle, vagrant and disorderly persons on work'. Nearly forty years later, they opened a second house at Manchester. But the Poor Law also recognised that there was a deserving poor. It made each parish responsible for the maintenance of its own sick, aged, very young, disabled, and mentally deranged. Justices were to ensure that overseers of the poor collected the parish poor rate and spent it on parishioners who could not help themselves. Quarter sessions' records contain hundreds of petitions drawing the attention of the justices to lame, sick, old or lunatic men and women who needed help. Many of these petitions were prompted or even drawn up by the overseers themselves, so that they could show that they were acting under the compulsion of a court order when fellow parishioners grumbled about the drain on the poor-rate funds. Begging licences, limited to a prescribed area, were occasionally granted to incurables, and parishes were frequently called on to finance a visit to London or elsewhere if there seemed hope of a cure. In 1672 Robert Butterworth of Castleton obtained help to go to London to be treated for cancer in the face, and in 1684 parishioners from Orrell, near Wigan, petitioned that Hugh Burrows should be allowed to go to Holywell to see if the waters could cure his blindness. The frequency of petitions to go to London for the cure of the king's evil showed a widespread faith in the power of the king's touch. Typical of such petitions is that of Richard Aspinall of Burscough, who asked that the overseers of the poor should grant money so that he could take to London a four-year-old boy, 'well nigh consumed with the king's evil'. The justices at the Ormskirk session granted £1, on the strict understanding that if the child died or for other reasons did not make the journey the money would be returned. The mentally sick were probably in the worst position, for no helpful treatment was ever attempted. The lunatic was treated as if he were a criminal. If the parish could not satisfactorily control him, he was sent to the house of correction, and the parish was charged with the cost of his maintenance.

A special problem of the years of the Interregnum and Restoration was the plight of the scores of men, who had been disabled in the wars, and, either immediately or eventually, were too crippled to earn their own living. In May 1647 John Fletcher of Prestwich, an ex-Parliamentary soldier, who had been shot through the left arm and right shoulder, petitioned quarter sessions at Manchester that the justices 'would be pleased to consider his low condition . . . and alow him sume place and timber in Pilkington, where he may live with his wife and children'. The court ordered that the churchwardens should provide him with a house. As late as 1673 John Hilton of Wheelton, between Chorley and Blackburn, appealed for help on the grounds that he had been one of Colonel Tyldesley's men, and at 'York Battle' had suffered no less than eighteen wounds, 'sixe in the head, in his armes and hands nine wounds, one wound in his side, another in his thigh and another in his leg, and did thereupon lye under the Surgeons hands one whole yeare the Cost and Charge whereof did much Impoverish the poore man'.

Hoghton Tower, abandoned by the family, 1710-1870

The acts of 1598 and 1601 could not always be rigorously applied. In years of scarcity, plague, or civil war, the justices had to intervene with such measures as fixing the price of corn, subsidising the sale of coal and charging the hundred with a special rate, thus attempting to relieve the worst distress, so that as many people as possible should be kept out of the house of correction. The Act of Settlement of 1662 forbade any stranger to settle in a parish unless he had means to rent a house worth £10 a year, or, alternatively, could find acceptable security that he would never be a charge on the poor rate of his adopted parish. This act was attempting to keep labour static just at the time when in Lancashire industrial and commercial changes were beginning to require a bigger movement of population than usual. Stricter amendments to the act made matters worse, until in 1697 a new act recognised the futility of insisting upon permanent settlement, and allowed people to seek work outside their own parish, providing that they carried a certificate guaranteeing that the parish would take responsibility if ever they became paupers. By the same act paupers were *badged,* and carried on their shoulder a clearly marked P followed by the initial letter of their original parish. This humilitating system dropped out of use in the eighteenth century, when the trickle of population movement in the Lancashire of Charles II and William III began to swell into a torrent.

But the Industrial Revolution brought with it new poor law problems of its own. Long before the end of the eighteenth century unskilled labour had become so cheap it was possible for a labourer to work a full week and not earn sufficient money to keep himself and his family fed and clothed. The justices had the power to fix wages at a higher rate, but they chose instead to authorise outdoor relief to supplement the inadequate wages. This method, known as the Speenhamland System, led to such abuse that eventually its evils were worse than those it had set out to cure.

Mar: 8th 1758 A True & Just Inventory of all the Goods & Chattles of the late Deceased James Horrocks of Bradshaw apprised & valued by us James Smith & James Kay

Goods in the House — £ S D.

A Dresser £2-5-0 Clock £2-0-0 — 4-5-0
A Coach Chair & Cushion 18s A White Table 1s 6d — 0-19-6
A Mapp 5s A Fire Iron & Crow & Tongs 18s — 1-03-0
6 Rush Chairs 7s Salt pye 1s A Tin Oven 2s 6d — 0-10-6
A Smoothing Iron & Heaters 3s Frying pan Bd Iron 1s 6d 0-4-6
Two Brass Candlesticks & an Iron one 2s 6d — 0-2-6
Chafing Dish 9d 1 Old Chair & 3 Stools 2:6d — 0-3-3
4 Boards 1s 3 Old Tresets & Bd Cloak 1s A Gun 2s 6d — 0-4-6
A Looking Glass 1s 3d Books 6d — 0-7-3

Goods in the Loom House —

A pair of Looms £1-0-0 A Steel Reed & other Geers — 6s 1-6-0

Goods in the Great Parlour —

A Cieled Chest 18s A Meal Chest £1-0-0 A Table 1s — 1-19-0

Part of a typical household inventory. Wills and probate inventories are valuable sources for social historians
By courtesy of the Lancashire Record Office.

XV *Lancashire as Others have seen her*

Bury Fold, Darwen, in mid-nineteenth century. Drawn by Charles Haworth, 1816-95

Old maps and contemporary descriptions of familiar places in times past rarely fail to rouse interest, because they offer a more picturesque way than most other documents to the understanding of local history. Their uses are limited but valuable. Lancashire shares with other counties the attentions of national cartographers and travellers, as well as having rich resources of her own.

Saxton's map of Lancashire (facing p. 41), with its curious sugar-loaf hills and its meticulous tracing of rivers but complete absence of roads, served as a model for later map-makers. Except that they marked the boundaries of the hundreds, neither John Speed's map of 1610 nor Blaeu's map (1645) nor the anonymous map of Lancashire dated 1680 added much to Saxton's data. These later maps were drawn more clearly, however, and Speed inserted into his top right-hand corner a town plan of Lancaster, and filled the Irish Sea and the Yorkshire side of the Pennines with portraits of the Lancastrian and Yorkist kings under the misconceived or admonitory title, *Blessed are the Peace-makers.* Morden's map, first published in 1676 and considerably revised in 1695, was the first county map to show the main roads. It owed its new information to John Ogilby, who in 1675 had published his strip-maps of the main English roads in his *Britannia . . . a Geographical and Historical Description of the Principal Roads thereof.* In 1752 Emanuel Bowen, engraver of maps to both George II and Louis XV, published a detailed map of Lancashire. He claimed he based it on 'the best authorities' but he did not re-survey the county. He used a bigger scale than previous map-makers (approximately one inch to three miles), but, instead of displaying more topographical details, he used the extra space to list gentlemen's houses and to print historical notes. Bowen published another edition of this popular map in 1780, but six years later it was completely outclassed by William Yates's map, the first 'modern' map of the county.

Yates surveyed Lancashire afresh, the first cartographer since Saxton to do so. He used the new triangulation technique, based on trigonometrical calculations, to establish the framework of his map, and then, in his own words, determined 'the directions and measures of the Roads, the Course of Rivers and Canals, and the situations of the intermediate parts by the Theodolite and Perambulator'. Yates's scale was one inch to the mile, and by using an elaborate key, he

Hand-tools for carding wool

distinguished between parliamentary boroughs, market towns which were not boroughs, parish centres and townships, as well as between rectories, vicarages and the different status of churches and chapels. On his roads he marked toll-gates and milestones, and on his canals locks. He showed the position of coal mines and water-driven machinery. His map is an indispensable guide to the industrial changes of the later eighteenth century, as Greenwood's (1818) and Hennett's (1829) maps are to the changes which took place in the years after the Napoleonic Wars. Hennett was so anxious that his map should be up-to-date that he marked on it as accomplished fact the Manchester-Liverpool railway, which was then only under construction, and even the St. Helens-Runcorn Gap railway, which was not opened for another four years. The six-inch ordnance survey map of Lancashire was completed in 1848, and, together with the tithe maps of different parishes, many of which date from the same decade, it offered far more local detail than any of the previous maps had attempted to do.

John Leland, official antiquary to Henry VIII, wrote thumb-nail sketches of Lancashire towns he visited about 1540. 'Wigan pavid, as bigge as Warington and better builded, there is one Paroch Church amidde the Towne, summe Marchauntes, sum Artificers, sum Fermers. Mr. Bradshaw hath a place caulled Hawe a Myle from Wigan. He hath founde moche Canal like Se Coole in his Grounde very profitable to him, and Gerade of Ynse dwellith in that paroch'. Leland was full of admiration for Manchester with its 'doble ilyd' collegiate church and its various stone bridges. He remarked on the 'praty little chapel' which stood on the three-arched Salford Bridge, which spanned the Irwell to join Manchester to Salford, its 'large suburbe'. Warrington he found to be 'a pavid town . . . of prety bygnes', Ormskirk a town with no river but mosses on every side, and the 'new toune' of Lancaster built hard by the ruins of an 'old place' in the descent from the castle. He commented upon such things as 'the wonderful poore or rather no market' at Chorley, the 'cottons and course Yarne' sold in Bolton market, the ruins of a castle alongside Bury parish church, and 'the great stone bridge of Rybill having a V. great arches', which he crossed on his way from Walton-le-dale to Preston. Leland's descriptions are mostly fleeting impressions of things which would quickly strike the observant visitor's eye, but, fifty years later, William Camden's observations occasionally go deeper. He noticed the unusual size of the Lancashire parishes, and, as Leland had done, journeyed through the mosses to lonely places on the coast to see salt-boilers at work in Amounderness, men going fishing with spades at Formby, and the deserted Cockersand Abbey 'exposed to the violence of the winds between the mouths of the Cocar and Lune'. He had an eye for

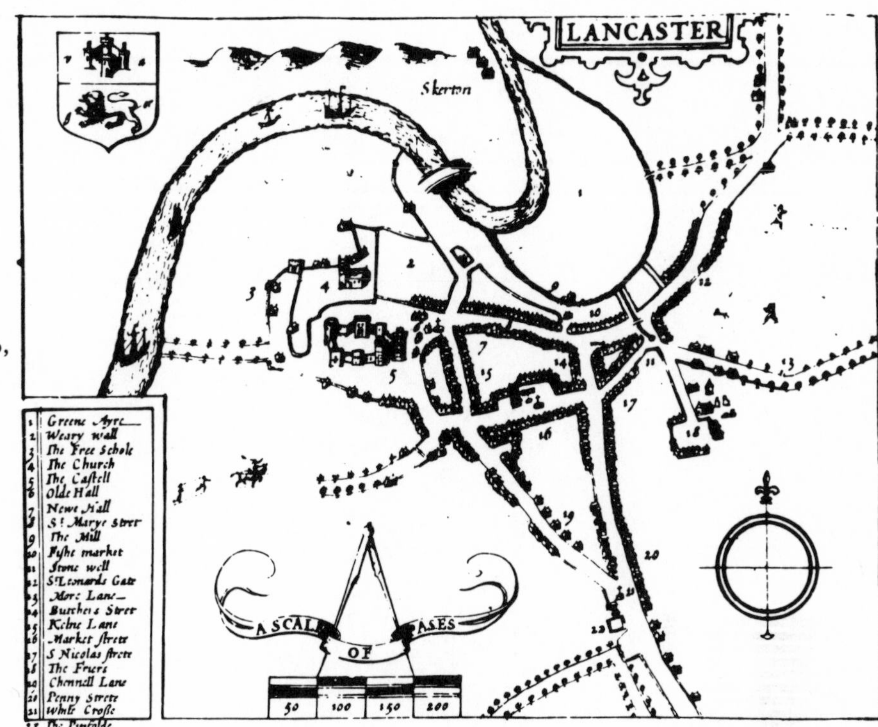

LANCASTER
Skerton
1 Greene Ayre
2 Weary wall
3 The Free Schole
4 The Church
5 The Castell
6 Olde Hall
7 Newe Hall
8 St Marye Strete
9 The Mill
10 Fyshe market
11 Stone well
12 St Leonards Gate
13 More Lane
14 Butchers Strete
15 Kelne Lane
16 Market strete
17 S Nicolas strete
18 The Friers
19 Chennell Lane
20 Penny Strete
21 White Crosse
22 The Pinfolde
A SCALE OF PASES
50 100 150 200

of Lancaster on Speed's map,

Rimington
Radholme park
Clothero
Colne
Mitton
Pendleton
Wiswall
Whaley
Stonyhurst
Longridg chap
Ribchester
Padium
Read hall
Harwood
Martholme
Shuttelworth
Townley
Hapton tower
Holme
Little Harwood
Samlesbery hall
Chirche
Blackborn
Hastingde
Darwen flu
Darwen chap
Irwel flu
Whitworth

Part of Blaeu's map of Lancashire 1645.

antiquities, for he enjoyed seeing the Roman remains at Ribchester, and he twice visited Samlesbury to read Roman inscriptions and admire an unusually well preserved Roman altar. The inscription carved on Winwick church in 'a barbarous old character' so intrigued him that he recorded it in full. Celia Fiennes, who in the last years of the seventeenth century rode on horseback through most of England, wrote chiefly about the state of the roads she used and of curiosities that intrigued her. From Halifax she came into Lancashire over 'the dismal high precipices' of Blackstone Edge, and then rode from Rochdale to Manchester between quickset hedges'cut smooth as even in a garden'. Her attention was caught by the enclosed fields which were so common in Lancashire, the high-arched bridges across the rivers, the novelty of seeing 'posts with Hands pointing to each road with the names of the great town or market towns that it leads to', the 'clap bread made all of oates' at Garstang, the new streets of Liverpool, the busy market and fine houses at Preston, and, probably more than by anything else, by the burning well 'which burns like brandy', which she visited near Wigan.

Many other visitors to Lancashire have recorded their impressions. In the reign of George I, Daniel Defoe in his *Tour through Great Britain* and, in 1770, Arthur Young in *Six Months' Tour through the North of England,* both threw on Lancashire isolated shafts of light, which occasionally reveal unexpected details and surprising contrasts. Defoe described Lancaster as lying in its own ruins with 'little to recommend it but a decayed castle, and a more decayed port'. But fifty years later Young saw handsome new buildings in the town, and a fleet of a hundred ships regularly bringing goods from Africa and America into the busy port, for he was visiting Lancaster in its first years of what its economic historian, M. M. Schofield, has called 'the golden age of Lancaster shipping'. Young had some biting things to say about Lancashire's roads. In his day, most turnpikes were not standing up to the increasing numbers and weight of industrial waggons and carts, but, in particular, he warned travellers to avoid 'the infernal road' north and south of Wigan 'as they would the devil'. He claimed he had measured ruts four feet deep, and added 'the only mending it in places receives, is the tumbling in some loose stones, which serve no other purpose but jolting a carriage in the most intolerable manner'. Samuel Derrick wrote a comprehensive description of Liverpool in 1760 in a letter to the earl of Cork, and Ann Radcliffe, in *Tour to the Lakes,* published in 1795, describes such different sights as the 'almost continued street of villages' from Stockport to Manchester, and 'the wide desolation of the sands' of Morecambe Bay. Such monumental topographical works as those of W. Watts and J. P. Neale on country

The ruins of the chapter house at Cockersand. S. and N. Buck, c. *1725*

houses and parks include Lancashire views and descriptions, and even Creevey's political papers are not without local interest; but for contemporary descriptions of eighteenth-century Lancashire the more detailed and specialised writings of J. Holt, T. D. Whittaker, T. West and J. Aikin cannot be surpassed.

William Roscoe 1753-1831

The atmosphere, as distinct from descriptions, of bygone Lancashire can be found more surely in the writings of Lancastrians, who were often doing no more than keeping a diary, penning verses or writing letters to friends. William Roscoe's stylised lines not only describe the development of Merseyside in the late eighteenth century, but also reveal the moral and political problems caused by the phenomenal increase in Liverpool's trade.

'Ah! why, ye Sons of Wealth, with ceaseless toil,
Add gold to gold, and swell the shining pile?
. . . thirst not with the same unconquer'd rage,
Till nature whitens in the frost of age;
But rather, on the present hour rely,
And catch the happier moments ere they fly.'

Autobiographies such as those of Adam Martindale and Henry Newcome help the reader to recapture the atmosphere of Puritan Lancashire, and the diaries of Nicholas Blundell of Little Crosby and William Stout of Lancaster, contemporary in date, do more than merely record the daily lives of two very different but equally energetic gentlemen in the early eighteenth century. Even the more prosaic *Itinerary of Dr. Kuerden* (1695) and *Diary of Ireland Greene* (mid-eighteenth century) have interest and usefulness. The blunt and often vituperative letters of Ellen Weeton, which for her were a personal vindication, are for the twentieth-century reader a means by which he can vicariously enjoy the slow journey by canal packet-boat from Gathurst to Liverpool, or holiday bathing on the shore at Kirkdale, or the hazards of travelling from Lancashire to North Wales, the English Lakes and the Isle of Man in the early years of last century. For life in textile Lancashire there is no richer source than the prose and verse, much of it in dialect, of John Collier (better known as Tim Bobbin), Samuel Bamford, Sam Laycock, Ben Brierley, Ammon Wrigley, Edwin Waugh, and, for the first half of this present century, T. Thompson. In the few verses of *Come, Mary, Link thi Arm i' Mine* Edwin Waugh expressed the kindly spirit of family and neighbourly co-operation, which, remarkable though it was, and still is, was taken for granted in the crowded streets of Lancashire's industrial towns.

'Eawr Tum has sent a bacon-flitch;
Eawr Jem a load o'coals:
Eawr Charlie's bought some pickters, an'
He's hanged 'em upo' th' woles;
Owd Posy's white-weshed th'cottage through;
Eawr Matty's made it sweet;
An Jack's gav me his Jarman flute,
To play bi' th'fire at neet.'

Numerous poems, such as Sam Laycock's well-known *Welcome, Bonny Brid,* bring reality into text-book accounts of the struggle for social and industrial reform in the nineteenth century.

'We've nobbut getten coarshish fare,
But eaut o' this tha'st ha' thi share,
    Never fear.
Aw hope tha'll never want a meel,
But allus fill thi bally weel.
    While tha'rt here.'

And Lancashire working-class resignation and philosophy is characteristically expressed in

'Owd time is a troublesome codger
Who keeps nudging us on to decay
While he whispers, "Tha'rt nobbut a lodger,
So get ready for pikin' away" '.

XVI The Port of Liverpool

During the Middle Ages the whole of the English coastline was divided into sections, and each section put under the administration of a chief port. Chester was chosen as the administrative centre of the north-west coast. Its safe anchorage and navigable river were attractive, and it was conveniently placed for controlling traffic between London and Ireland. Chester's jurisdiction covered the long coastline from Barmouth to Solway Firth, and the harbours at Beaumaris, Caernarvon, Liverpool, Poulton and Lancaster were recognised as 'creeks' or lesser ports, in which assistants of the Chester port officers had to reside. These officers, the customer, the comptroller and the searcher, were royal officials responsible for levying and collecting customs duties and safeguarding the king's interests. Local port dues were levied by the separate ports themselves, and collected by local officials.

From the sixteenth to the early nineteenth century, Liverpool had dozens of windmills

In the first half of the fifteenth century the sandbanks in the Dee estuary shifted so that the river was partially blocked. Small ships could still sail to Chester, but bigger ships had to unload their goods in the Hyle or Hoyle Lake, and transfer them by pack-horse to the port. Time made matters worse, but there was little immediate concern because the weakness of English government in Ireland had caused Irish trade to shrink and had made the Irish Sea most unsafe for shipping. Once Henry VII and Henry VIII had restored order on the seas and in Ireland, however, the Chester merchants were eager to enjoy all they could get of the reviving trade. In 1553 the Merchant Venturers of Chester established themselves as a chartered company, and between 1541 and 1578, at the cost of about £6,000, the city of Chester constructed a 'New Haven' at Neston. Ships of about seventy tons could sail up the Dee as far as this, and if the goods were intended for the Midlands or for London, it was still cheaper to bring them into the Dee than into the Mersey.

But at the very time that Chester was trying to overcome its difficulties a new trade was steadily developing with Ireland. The growing textile industry in south-east Lancashire required Irish flax to mix with the wool from the Pennines, and it was able to pay for this by exporting fabrics to Ireland. The shipowners of Liverpool could handle this trade better than the Chester merchants. Their little ships, never more than forty tons and often much less, could enter the smaller Irish ports and sail their cargoes up the Mersey as far as Runcorn.

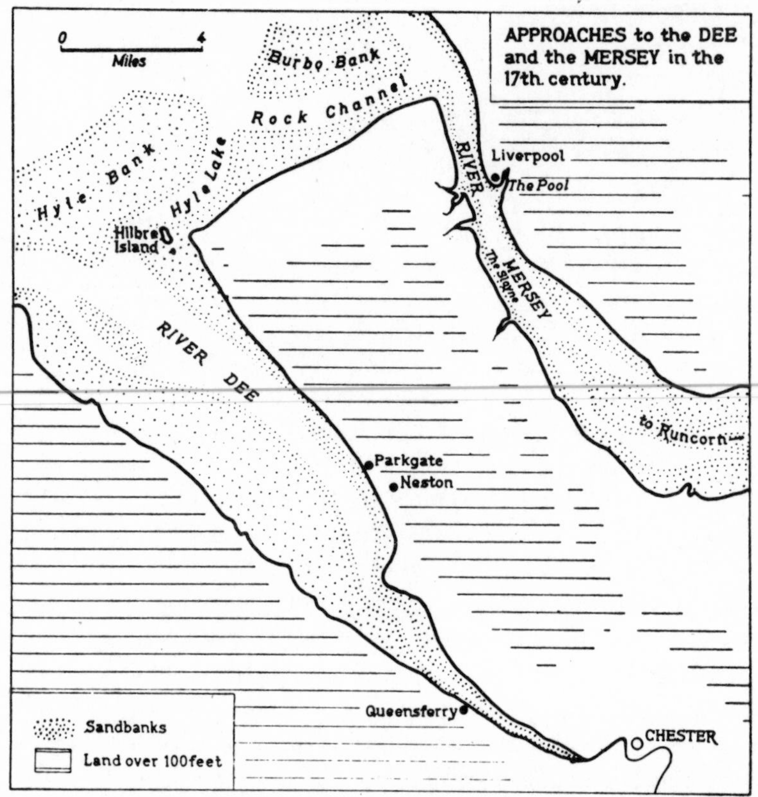

Lower port charges helped to make the Mersey popular, and the Liverpool owner-masters gradually attracted export cargoes of coal, salt, and metal work from south Lancashire and north Cheshire, and brought back into the Mersey wool, hides and skins as well as flax from Ireland. 'Irish merchants come much thither as to a good haven', wrote John Leland in Henry VIII's reign, and in 1590 William Camden described the Mersey as the 'most commodious and frequented' passage to Ireland. In 1561 and again in 1577 the harbourage of the Pool was repaired and improved, so that more ships could be accommodated at a time. But it is easy to get a false impression of the size of Liverpool's trade. Throughout the sixteenth and first half of the seventeenth century Liverpool's seven streets had less than three hundred houses, and less than a score of ships were owned by Liverpool merchants. Chester's population was considerably bigger, but in Elizabeth's reign her merchants did no more trade than Liverpool's sailors. The customs returns for 1586 show that out of £483 paid by Chester and her creeks Liverpool paid £272, about 56 per cent. Little wonder that the Liverpool shipowners resisted strongly when in 1580, the Merchant Venturers of Chester tried to extend their control of trade to Chester's

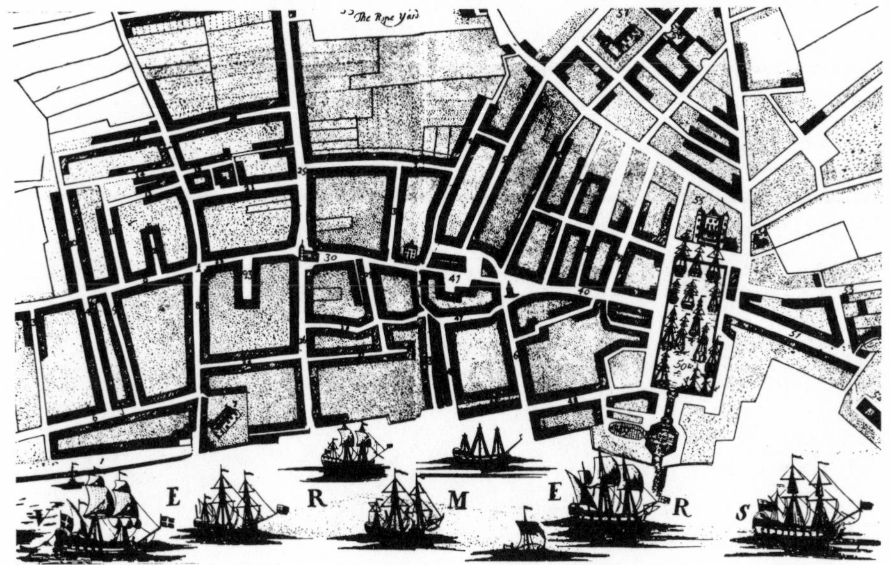

Above: Chadwick's Map, 1725, shows the first dock built in the mouth of the Pool
Below: Eyes's Map, 1765, shows the town's growth in the next forty years.
(Both maps are reproduced on the same scale)

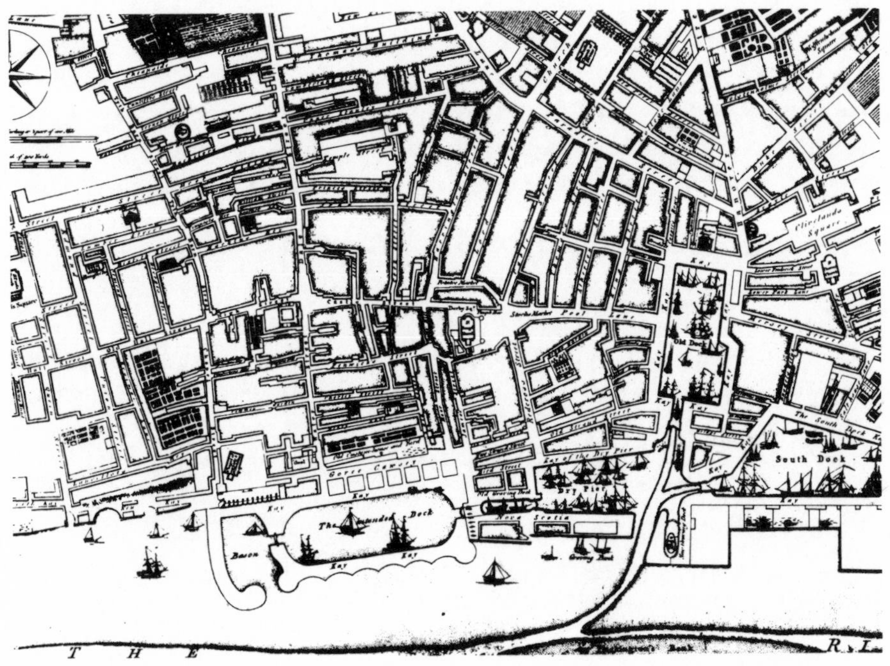

Liverpool's Second Customs House

creeks. They maintained that Liverpool should be considered as a 'member port' and not a dependent creek, and, with the official backing of the common council of Liverpool, claimed that Liverpool should control all Mersey shipping whether sailing to or from the Cheshire or the Lancashire shore. The Master of the Rolls, before whom the case was heard, decided for Liverpool, but this verdict did not end the dependence of Liverpool on Chester for the control of customs. In 1660 a boundary stone was set up at the mouth of the Dee to divide the 'liberties' of Chester from the 'liberties' of Liverpool, and eleven years later, when the authority of the ports was re-defined, Liverpool was given responsibility for the collection of customs on both banks of the Mersey and along the coast of West Derby hundred. The royal officers at Liverpool were still assistants to those at Chester even at the end of the seventeenth century, but by that time Liverpool's trade was considerably bigger than Chester's, and the dispute had ceased to be of practical importance.

The Irish Rebellion of 1641, the English Civil Wars and Cromwell's 1649 campaign in Ireland all damaged the Irish trade, which was so important to Liverpool. Only after the Restoration of Charles II did it show signs of revival, and in anticipation of new profits Liverpool owners built a dozen new ships. But the Cavalier Parliament added to the Navigation Laws, which sought to regulate imports and exports, a series of detailed measures forbidding English traders to import Irish livestock and dairy products. The Irish were compelled to sell to, and therefore to buy from, other European countries, and trade between England and Ireland was rapidly reduced to a tenth of what it had been. This was one of the reasons why Liverpool shipowners began to seek new markets further afield. On 15 September 1666, *The Antelope,* financed by a number of Liverpool men, sailed out of the Mersey bound for Barbados. This ship of about sixty tons, the first that is definitely known to have made a trans-Atlantic crossing from Liverpool and back, carried a mixed cargo worth about £200, of which 3,332 yards of linen cloth valued at £130 15s. 9d. was easily the biggest single item. Shoes, slippers, nails, spikes and coal made up the rest. On 19 August 1667 *The Antelope,* laden with sugar, sailed safely back into the Mersey, and those who had financed her received double their investment when the profits were shared. This successful pioneer voyage encouraged others. *The Lamb* and *The Providence* returned from ventures in 1669, and ten years later half a dozen Liverpool ships had become regular traders with Barbados. In 1667 Allyn Smith, a London manufacturer, had the foresight to build a sugar refinery off Dale Street, Liverpool. It must have made a fortune, but tobacco cargoes from Virginia were soon even more profitable than sugar from

9 and 30. Two Regency Market-places. (*above*) Preston (*below*) Wigan.

31 and 32. Two Lancashire Prisons. (*above*) The New Bayley and River Irwell, Salford, *c.* 1800. The prison was named after Thomas B. Bayley, a local magistrate, who laid the foundation stone in 1787. The building was demolished in 1871. (*below*) The Tower at Liverpool, founded by Sir Thomas Lathom in the fourteenth century and fortified by the Stanleys soon after 1400. From *c.* 1740 until *c.* 1810 the Town Council used it as a gaol. The last of the building was pulled down in 1821 for the widening of Water Street.

Barbados. During the last twenty years of the seventeenth century Liverpool business progressed remarkably. Much of the Irish trade was recovered, and increasing demands for Cheshire salt and Lancashire textiles, coal, pottery and metal goods sent her new ships of 200–300 tons to many west-European ports as well as across the Atlantic. In 1699 the mayor and aldermen proudly claimed that Liverpool was now 'the third port of the trade of England and pays upwards of £50,000 [in customs] *per annum* to the king'.

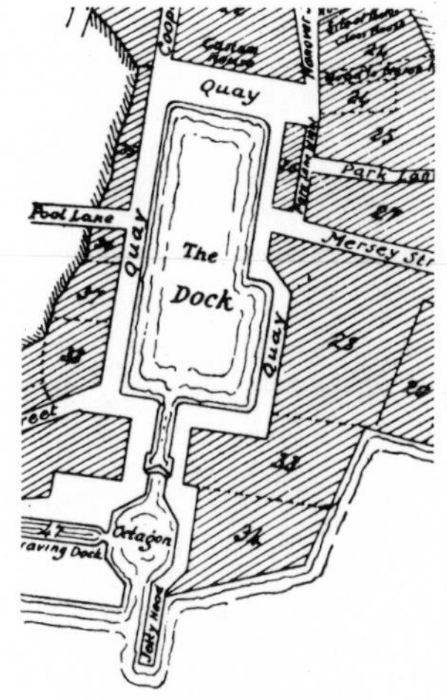

Liverpool's first dock. Land reclaimed from the Pool is shaded

Before 1660 Liverpool's population had never been more than about 1,500 people. By 1708 it had increased to about 6,000, and the streets from seven to over thirty. When Chadwick drew his well-known plan in 1725, the town had spread outwards from the river along Tithebarn Street, Dale Street, Church Street, and Hanover Street. Visitors could not help but remark both on the rate of expansion and on the handsome buildings that were being erected. About 1705 Defoe described Liverpool as 'one of the wonders of Britain', because, since he had last visited the town in 1690, he was convinced it had more than doubled in size.

Liverpool ships loaded and unloaded in the Pool, a sheltered, shallow, tidal tributary of the Mersey. But when ships were built bigger and in greater numbers the Pool became too small and inconvenient. The strong tides made the Mersey itself, except on the Sloyne off Tranmere, unsafe for anchorage, and before the end of the seventeenth century the bigger ships were unloading part of their cargo in the Hoyle Lake, and more of the smaller ships were sailing up the river to Runcorn and Warrington to unload. The loss of several anchored ships in a great gale in 1703 finally convinced the common council that it was necessary to build a dock. Several schemes were considered, and in 1710 Thomas Steers's plan to build a four-acre dock in the mouth of the Pool was accepted. Five years later, the dock, which could hold about one hundred small ships, was in use, and soon afterwards the rest of the Pool was filled in. The present Paradise Street and Whitechapel mark its original course. One dock, however, did not suffice for long. In 1738 Steers began to construct Salthouse Dock, but in its last stages he handed over the work to his successor, Henry Berry, who by 1771 had built George's Dock on the site of the present Liver Buildings, and by 1788 King's Dock to the south of Salthouse. Before the end of the century Queen's Dock stood alongside King's Dock, and the five basins, administered by the common council, received nearly 5,000 ships, or more than 450,000 tons of shipping a year. Trade and town increased together. A 'survey' of 1773 gave the number of inhabitants as 34,407, a 'scrutiny' of 1790 as 53,853, and the first census in 1801 as 77,653. Liverpool's houses were spreading

On the dock-side

rapidly towards Toxteth Park in the south, beyond Mount Pleasant towards Edge Hill in the east, and northwards through Scotland Road and Vauxhall Road towards the residential areas of Kirkdale and Everton.

Part of Liverpool's eighteenth-century wealth came from the African trade and from privateering in time of war. Privateers such as Fortunatus Wright and William Hutchinson brought captive into the Mersey valuable ships and cargoes, but these spectacular gains had to be balanced against losses suffered at the hands of foreign privateers and the harmful effects of war conditions on normal trade. Steadier profits were made by ships engaged in slaving, a business which was a natural expansion of Liverpool's West Indian trade. Once the Royal Africa Company lost its monopoly of trade with Africa in 1697, Liverpool shipowners took an increasing part in slave-trading. Their first ships were some of the smaller vessels previously used for carrying sugar and tobacco. In 1700 *Liverpool Merchant,* about 80 tons at most, carried 220 negroes from Africa to Barbados, where they were sold for £4,239. But once the trade was seen to be profitable, Liverpool merchants built special ships of 300 tons or more, well-armed and designed for speed. On the outward journey they carried cargoes of cloth, clothes, shoes, spirits, household utensils, and personal ornaments, which were bartered for slaves at several places along the Guinea coast. As soon as they were fully slaved the Guineamen set sail for the West Indies, for their captains were anxious to keep alive below decks as many slaves as possible on the fifty days' voyage. In Jamaica or Barbados the human cargo was sold at a good profit, and then the ships, laden with sugar, tobacco or molasses, sailed back to Liverpool. In a good year more than a hundred ships made this profitable triangular journey, and most Liverpool men shut their ears to the rising clamour against trading in human souls. William Roscoe, the Liverpool poet, scholar, merchant and politician, made himself very unpopular when he published his poem, *The Wrongs of Africa,* in 1787.

'O Albion, say, . . . Blush ye not
To boast your equal laws, your just restraints,
Your rights defin'd, your liberties secur'd,
Whilst with an iron hand ye crush to earth
The helpless African; and bid him drink
That cup of sorrow, which yourself have dash'd
Indignant, from oppression's fainting grasp?'.

But he continued to speak and write in favour of the anti-slavery movement, and in 1807, as M.P. for Liverpool, had the satisfaction of voting for the bill which abolished the slave trade.

Steam ferries on the Mersey c. *1825*

Far from ruining Liverpool's livelihood, the end of the slave trade marked the beginning of a long period of exceptional prosperity. Progressively during the first half of the nineteenth century, Britain found new markets in South America, Africa, and the Far East, and Liverpool was well placed to export the textiles, machinery, chemicals, and metal goods which the new customers required. The port rapidly expanded. In the next century and a quarter, the thirty acres of water enclosed by the five eighteenth-century docks grew to over 650 acres enclosed in ninety-eight docks and basins, most of which are separated from the river by a protective granite wall eleven feet thick. From 1825 to 1857 the docks were managed by a Dock Committee, on which merchants and shipowners were the most active members. The chief engineer was an energetic, single-minded Yorkshireman, Jesse Hartley. Between 1824 and 1860, Hartley kept the whole of the port facilities in good repair and built more than twenty new docks. Their names—Canning, Huskisson, Clarence, Victoria, Albert, and others—proclaim the period in which they were built. This mammoth achievement, however, might have been in vain but for the work of Henry Denham of the hydrographical section of the Royal Navy. In the mid-1830s he discovered, dredged, and buoyed the New Channel through the sandbanks of Liverpool Bay, and so made Liverpool's shipping independent of the traditional Rock and Formby Channels, both of which were steadily silting up.

In 1857 Parliament replaced the Dock Committee by the Mersey Docks and Harbour Board. All but four of the members of the Board were representatives of the merchants and shipowners who used the port, and, with a will, they continued the expansion policy of the old Committee. By 1900 they had opened nine new docks in Liverpool and Bootle, and two in Birkenhead. Such docks as Canada and Alexandra Docks were much bigger than the older docks higher up the river, but even they were outclassed by Gladstone Dock which the Board opened in 1927 to accommodate the biggest ships afloat. In 1972 the Board completed the even bigger Seaforth Dock to handle the new container traffic. To ensure the success of all this expansion, the Board, by constant dredging and by building training walls to hold back the sand, has kept open the Mersey channels so that the biggest ships can enter and leave the port at any state of the tide. This long-lived success made it hard to believe the news when early in the 1970s, the Board encountered severe financial trouble.

XVII The Lancashire Textile Industry

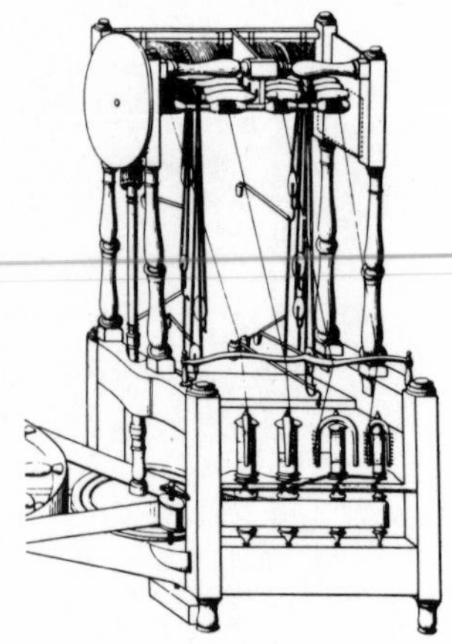

Arkwright's Water Frame

Though Leland described Manchester, about 1540, as 'the fairest best buildid, quickkest and most populus tounne of al Lancastreshire', he said nothing about the industrial activity which made it so. But Camden, who first visited the town in 1586, wrote in his book *Britannia,* that 'in the last age' Manchester, which was then manufacturing woollen cloth, had been 'much more famous for its manufacture of stuffs called Manchester cottons'. Leland said that the villages round Bolton 'do make cottons', and an act of 1552 sought to regulate the length and weight of 'Manchester and Lancashire cottons and Manchester rugs and friezes'. The word *cottons* has frequently led to misunderstanding. Leland and Camden used it to denote coarse woollen cloths, though after the Levant Company had begun to import cotton-wool from Cyprus, Smyrna and other places in the eastern Mediterranean, Lancashire weavers did use cotton yarn for the weft of some of their fabrics. They used linen or wool for the much longer warp yarns, and it was not until after the invention of power spinning machines about 1770 that it was possible extensively to manufacture cloth entirely from cotton yarn.

Occasional and indirect references to textile manufacture in south-east Lancashire have been found in manuscripts as early as the late thirteenth century. By the Tudor period the industry was both lively and well organised. Merchants or 'clothiers' bought the raw wool, flax, and (later) cotton, distributed it to be spun and woven on hand spinning-wheels and hand-operated looms in scores of cottages, collected the cloth, and then had it finished, dyed and marketed. Many clothiers, mercers, and drapers took some part in manufacture as well as in buying raw material and selling finished products. Most of them were relatively humble men. None were so rich as John Lacy or Nicholas Mosley, two London merchants, who, in 1579 and 1596 respectively, purchased the manor of Manchester simply because they were financially interested in the textile trade.

At first the wool used in south-east Lancashire came from sheep reared on the slopes of the Pennines, and the flax from the low-lying country round Rufford and Croston. But these supplies became insufficient, and by the sixteenth century Irish flax and wool were being imported in increasing quantities. Although each area of south Lancashire specialised in particular types of textiles, the county manufactured a wide variety of cloths, and a steadily increasing sale was found for them in the London market and abroad. Mercer's shops could stock a bewildering assortment of textiles, with a wide range of prices and colours. When Matthew Markland, a Wigan mercer, died in 1617, he left on the shelves of his shop rolls of more than twenty-five different kinds of cloth, many in two or three colours, and at prices ranging from sackcloth at 6d. and fustian at 1s. a yard, to very expensive cloths such as stammel, a fine, red, woollen cloth at 12s. 6d. and russets varying from 6s. 8d. to 13s. a yard. The Puritans favoured perpetuana, a close-woven material which cost about 2s. 4d. a yard; and for those who wanted something gayer but not too dear, there was yellow buffine at 1s. 2d. or red durant at 1s. 4d. a yard. Some of Markland's stock came from further afield, but most of it had been manufactured in south Lancashire.

Samuel Crompton

During the seventeenth century this cottage industry developed steadily but unspectacularly. By 1700 each district was specialising in the production of one type of cloth more than another. The Preston area and the towns and villages round Stockport and Ashton-under-Lyne produced almost all the linen cloth made. Bolton and Blackburn were centres for fustians, and most woollens and worsteds were manufactured in Bury, Rochdale, Burnley and Colne. The eighteenth century, however, witnessed not only big increases in the production of these traditional textiles, but also the development of cotton cloth manufacture. Between 1741 and 1750 Lancashire spinners and weavers doubled their annual consumption of raw cotton. By 1780 they had doubled it again, and between 1780 and 1787 their annual requirements jumped from five to twenty-two million pounds weight. The years of the French wars did little to retard this remarkable rate of development.

New machines which used power and necessitated the steady replacement of the domestic system by the factory system of manufacture achieved this textile revolution. 'The English are uncommonly dextrous in their contrivance of the mechanic powers', wrote Josiah Tucker in 1757, and certainly in the eighteenth century England led the world in mechanical inventions. The earliest spinning patent was registered in 1678, but power spinning on a large scale did not become possible until after 1779 when Crompton invented the Mule. This was an improvement on Hargreaves's Spinning Jenny—a hand-operated, domestic machine—which in 1765 had itself made a notable advance on Paul's Spinning Machine first patented in 1738. Arkwright's Water Frame, invented ten years before the Mule, adapted Paul's invention for the spinning of cotton warps. Kay improved the hand loom with his Flying Shuttle as early as 1733, but Cartwright's

Hargreaves' Spinning Jenny

mechanical loom was not invented until 1787. Even then it suffered so many teething troubles that it did not seriously challenge the hand loom for another generation. The power first used for spinning machines was water power supplied by the fast-flowing Pennine streams, but Watt's steam engine later offered a more reliable source of power. After 1789, when Boulton and Watt first set up one of their engines in Drinkwater's mill in Manchester, the new source of power was slowly adopted at first for spinning and more gradually for weaving.

Mills in Lower Darwen, mid-nineteenth century. Drawn by Charles Haworth, 1816-95

These inventions were most unpopular in Lancashire. Both Kay and Hargreaves had their machines destroyed, and Arkwright as a safety measure had to spread the report in Preston that he was designing a machine to measure longitude. The craftsmen mistrusted the new machines partly because the expense of buying them made the detested factory system inevitable, and partly because the new machine-made yarn and cloth could easily undersell the products of the hand spinning-wheel and loom. The merchants who organised domestic labour were equally fearful of competition. Difficult times were blamed on the new machines, and this hostility together with the cost of erection slowed up the conversion of the industry to power. As late as the 'twenties and 'thirties of the nineteenth century hand-loom weavers were still in a majority in Lancashire, and still able to make a living against machine competition. Similarly water power persisted far longer than is generally imagined. In May 1861 John O'Neil, a Clitheroe weaver, wrote in his diary, 'Ribble is very low and in the afternoon our looms go very slow for want of water', and in the following November he complained, 'Ribble is so high that we had to stop half-an-hour sooner for backwater'.

By the beginning of the nineteenth century cotton had almost entirely replaced wool and linen in Lancashire mills. The southern states of North America, the port of Liverpool and south-east Lancashire were combined in a most profitable industrial and commercial enterprise. In 1820 Lancashire exported about 290 million yards of cotton cloth. Forty years later that annual figure had risen to 2,000 million yards. But in 1861 civil war broke out in the United States. The northerners blockaded the southern ports, and thus stopped the supply of cotton to Lancashire. For four years cotton workers endured very hard conditions. Surat cotton from India was an insufficient and unsatisfactory substitute for American cotton, and charitable effort could do no more than alleviate the worst of the suffering. But once the American war was over, Lancashire quickly recovered and trade again increased. By the end of the century the export figure had reached 5,000 million yards, and the industry was employing more than half a million workers. Just before war broke out in 1914, the export figure reached the record of 6,600 million yards, and throughout the war years the machines clattered and banged without ceasing.

After the 1914–18 war prospects for the future seemed to be even brighter. Share-values rocketed surprisingly, until the 1920 slump ruined many speculators and mill-owners. Textile Lancashire has never fully recovered from this blow, and competition from Japan and India has made matters worse. Between the wars trade shrank. Hundreds of operatives left the mill towns to seek work elsewhere, and today many old cotton mills are equipped to produce other things, from wireless parts and biscuits to canned vegetables and soups. Even those that still manufacture textiles are more concerned with man-made fibres than with cotton.

Manchester's second Exchange, 1809-74

XVIII Turnpikes, Canals and Early Railways

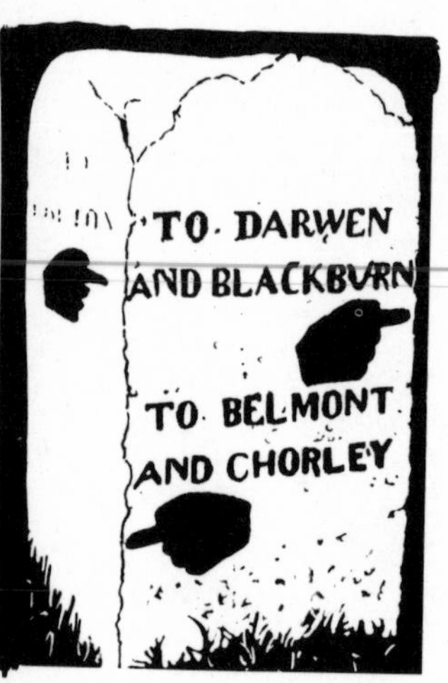

Pre-turnpike Fingerpost

The Highways Act of 1555 made each parish responsible for the maintenance of its own roads and bridges. Every year two or more parishioners were appointed surveyors of the highways. Under the superintendence of the justices of the peace, they had to see that all householders worked on the local roads for four (later six) days a year, and that landowners provided carts, oxen or horses, tools and labourers for a similar period. From 1691 the parish was entitled to supplement this amateur and haphazard labour by hired labour paid for by a highway rate; but because of a natural reluctance to pay rates few parishes took advantage of this new act. Not until 1835 was statute labour abolished and replaced by regular labour financed by a general highway rate. Most Lancashire parishes were exceptionally big, and responsibility for the long stretches of main road which ran through parishes such as Winwick and Lancaster disheartened the parishioners. Lancashire roads became notorious in an England in which muddy and rutted roads were accepted as normal. Oliver Cromwell described the road between Preston and Wigan as 'twelve miles of such ground as I never rode in all my life', and Richard James, a seventeenth-century Lancashire poet, wrote,

'Our wayes are gulphs of durt and mire, which none
Scarce ever passe in summer withoute moane.'

In 1628 Quarter Sessions permitted Chorley parish to put chain barriers across its roads in unfavourable weather in order to compel 'strangers and passeingers' to fetch 'their coales and other necessaries in faire and houldsome weather, or else not'. Neither such an attitude of mind nor such roads could answer the challenge of even the first stages of the Industrial Revolution, when speedier communication was becoming increasingly necessary, and when pack-horse, cart and waggon had bigger and more frequent loads to carry from mine to workshop and from workshop to market or port. The men of the eighteenth century solved this problem of transport by turnpiking the roads, widening and dredging rivers, and, later, constructing canals: the men of the nineteenth century built railways, which took over the long-distance communication hitherto maintained by roads, and eventually deprived the canals of almost all their business.

The movable wooden barrier at the tollhouse gave the name *turnpike* to the new roads. An act of Parliament made each turnpike trust, or committee of local gentlemen, responsible for keeping its particular road in good repair. It set out in detail the charges it could make for the use of the road; for example, waggons with four horses, 1s. 6d.; coaches, 1s.; chaises, 6d.; cattle, ½d; and sheep, ¼d. The trust employed professional surveyors and regular road-workers. Wherever possible they shortened the original road, widened the narrow strip of cobble stones that had been 'the horse causeway', and with crushed stones and sometimes industrial waste re-surfaced the cartway. Road engineering steadily improved. Originally each turnpike had a specific purpose, such as making possible all-weather transport of coal from the Prescot and St. Helens mines to Liverpool, or the easier transport of yarn and cloth in and out of Manchester, but the criss-cross of new roads which soon developed made travelling faster and more pleasant throughout the whole of the county. From 1760 onwards regular stage-coach services carrying passengers and mail plied between the main Lancashire towns and London. In the early years of George III's reign Liverpolitans had the choice of travelling to London in two or three days—according to the weather—by the Flying Machine for £2 6s. 0d., or taking the journey much more steadily and sedately in the Old and Constant Stage Waggons, which did the journey in four days. Manchester's London service set out from the *Royal Oak* in Market Street on Mondays and Thursdays, reached Derby the first night, Northampton the second, and London the third. The cost was £2 5s. 0d. for each passenger who travelled inside. 'Outside Passengers and Children on Lap to pay half price', and each passenger could take fourteen pounds weight of luggage. Before 1800 daily coach services linked all the main towns in Lancashire with one another, with Scotland, and with Yorkshire, and the Midlands. But costs were high. A journey from Manchester to Rochdale cost 5s., from Preston to Lancaster, 6s., and from Liverpool to Edinburgh, £5.

Pickford's Depot at Liverpool, c. *1800*

Water transport did not increase the speed of travel, but barges and flats (barges with sails) could carry bulk materials, such as coal, salt, stone and timber, which were difficult and uneconomic to transport by road. The Mersey between Runcorn and Warrington (1694), the Douglas (1719), the Upper Mersey and Irwell (1720), and the Weaver (1730) were the first rivers in the north-west to be shortened, widened, and dredged for regular industrial traffic. In 1755 Berry, the Liverpool engineer, set about making the Sankey Brook navigable enough for barges to be able to carry to Liverpool much-needed coal from the pits south-east of St. Helens. The Sankey had too little water for the usual type of 'navigation', so Berry persuaded John Ashton, the chief promoter, that a *cut* or canal separate from the Sankey would be a better solution. Two years later, England's first industrial canal, officially known as the Sankey Navigation, was in operation. It was so successful that more canals quickly followed. By 1761 the Duke of Bridgewater had his canal carrying coal from Worsley to Manchester. Twelve years later he had extended that canal to join the Mersey at Runcorn. In 1774 Liverpool and Wigan were linked by canal: later, in the early nineteenth century, this canal was carried *over* the Pennines to Leeds. During the early 1790s Manchester became the hub of a group of canals connecting the cotton capital to Bury, Bolton, Oldham, Rochdale, and, finally in 1794, *through* the Pennines to Huddersfield. In the same decade the Lancaster Canal established a promising link between north and south Lancashire. Canals had quickly become the pride and wonder of the new industrial age.

James Brindley, canal engineer

Railways began life as the handmaidens of canals: trucks, pulled along rails by horses or by ropes and standing steam-engines, carried coal or stone from the mine or quarry to the canal basin. But once the engineers had created the heavy locomotive, railways steadily replaced canals. In the early 1820s, merchants in Liverpool and Manchester were considering plans for a railway between their two towns. In 1825 the Liverpool and Manchester Railway Company promoted the necessary parliamentary bill. The canal companies, local landowners, and even Liverpool Corporation fought against the bill, and Parliament rejected it. The next year, the railway company submitted an amended bill. This time it passed, and in September 1830 the Duke of Wellington formally opened the line from Edge Hill to Manchester, the first public railway in the world. The engineer was George Stephenson. His greatest achievement was to carry the line successfully across the treacherous Chat Moss. But it was probably the enthusiasm and energy of Henry Booth, the secretary of the company, that did most to create this railway.

During the next twenty years gangs of hard-working 'navvies' created a network of public railways all over the county. Warrington, Bolton, Leigh, Wigan, and St. Helens were quickly linked to the Liverpool-Manchester line. By 1840 there were lines from Preston to Wigan, to Lancaster, to Fleetwood and to Longridge, and during the next ten years were built most of the main lines in the textile area of the county. The first line in Furness—from Dalton to Barrow and Roa Island—opened in 1846, but not until 1857 was it possible to travel by rail from Furness, through Carnforth, to the rest of Lancashire.

XIX Coal-mining and Metal Industries

Records of coal-mining in the Colne area go back at least as far as the thirteenth century, but not until Tudor times did any extensive mining begin in Lancashire. Leland wrote of cannel-mining at Haigh near Wigan, and during Elizabeth's reign land-owners were speculating in coal-bearing land, and safeguarding mineral rights when they leased land for farming. Wigan, Prescot, Hulton-Worsley and the Calder valley were the chief centres of this mining of thin seams relatively near the surface. Wherever the coal seam cropped out on a hillside, the colliers got at it by digging a sloping tunnel along the line of the seam. They cut the coal as they steadily penetrated the earth and dragged it in boxes to the mouth of the mine. Where *drift mines* such as these were not possible, the colliers sank vertical shafts to the coal seam, and then dug out coal until the *bee-hive* was in danger of collapsing. A series or *rank* of bee-hive mines was often sunk to the same seam. Drainage was always a serious problem, but firedamp was controlled by lowering a lighted candle or burning brasier into the empty mine before work for the day began. Since 1945 the mechanical excavators of the open-cast miner have worked (more efficiently, if more devastatingly) many of the same coal-deposits as the picks and spades of the seventeenth-century collier.

Early nineteenth-century machine-making factory near Bolton

The invention of the steam-engine increased considerably the industrial demand for coal, and at the same time enabled the coal miner to sink shafts to the deeper and thicker seams. A Newcomen engine was being used for pumping on the Prescot coalfield as early as 1719, but only in the nineteenth century did deep coal-mining in Lancashire really begin. Boulton and Watt or, later, Cornish beam steam-engines worked the pumps, the winding gear and the ventilator fans, and Davy's lamps ensured greater safety underground. The depths of shafts steadily increased from the 500 feet considered to be *deep* in the later eighteenth century. In 1869 the Rosebridge pit at Wigan was sunk to almost 2,500 feet. In 1904 the Pendleton colliery reached about 3,500 feet, and Parsonage colliery, Leigh, has worked seams 4,000 feet deep. Until 1914 Lancashire's coal mines employed an ever-growing number of colliers. In the first years of the twentieth century, some 87,000 men were producing some 25,000,000 tons annually. But since the first world war, production has shrunk. Seams have run out or become uneconomic to mine. Waste heaps covered with rough

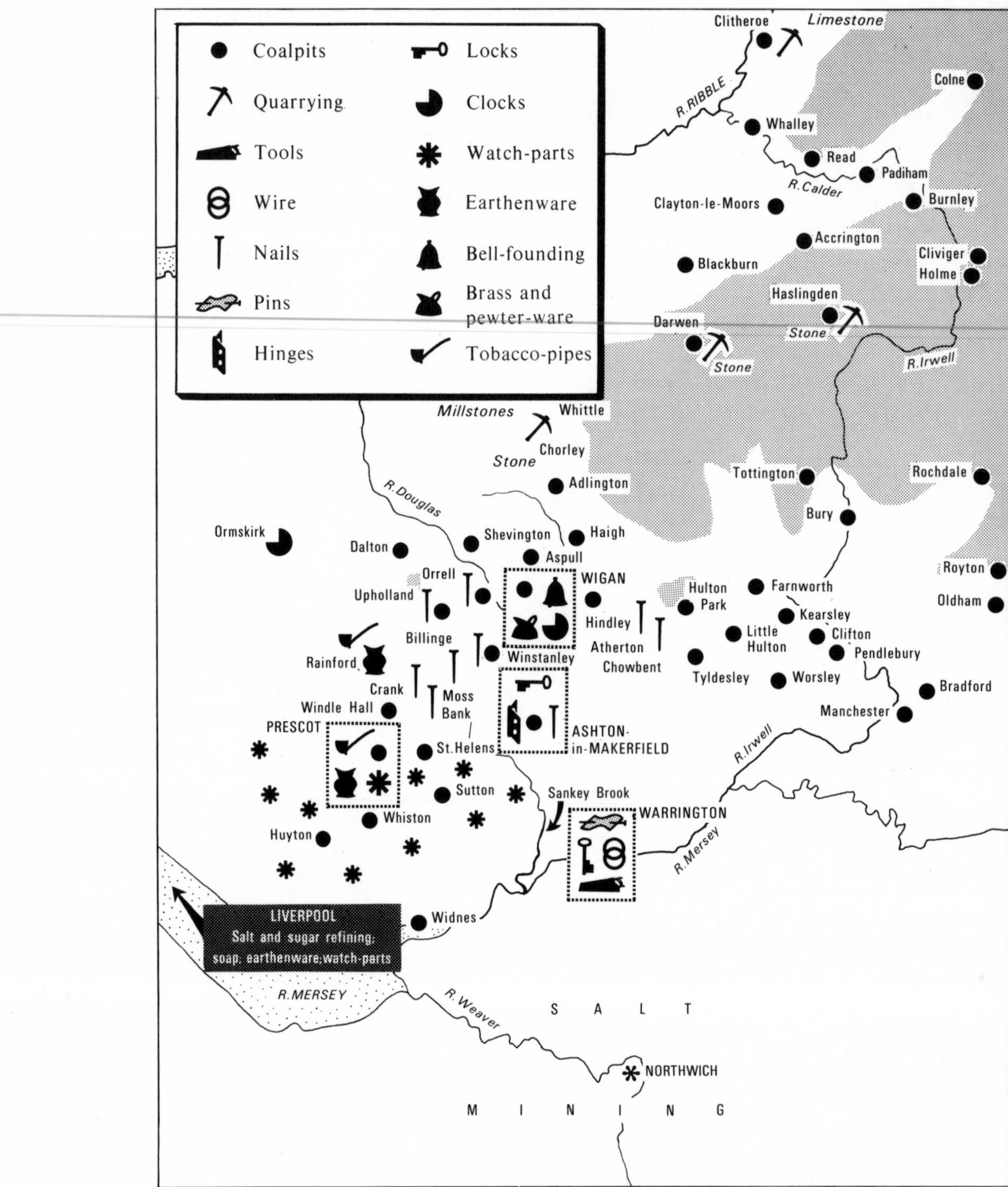

Mining and Metal Industries, *c.* 1725

grass mark the sites of many abandoned pits and those collieries still working produce less than half the county's pre-1914 tonnage.

Tower of St. George's, Everton, one of the first churches to use cast iron for pillars, arches and decoration. 1812-14

During the Middle Ages, most iron smelting in Lancashire was done in Furness, where ore could be easily mined and the woodlands of High Furness could provide the necessary charcoal. Lesser iron-producing districts were Simonswood, Rossendale, Quernmore, and the country between Garstang and Bleasdale Moor. The iron produced by the bloomeries in all these places might be of poor quality, but from Tudor times onwards it was in rapidly increasing demand for making nails, locks, hinges, clock and watch parts, and many kinds of tools. Nail-makers in the villages to the south-east and south-west of Wigan, lock and hinge-makers round Ashton-in-Makerfield, watch-part makers in south-west Lancashire, all built their forges alongside their cottages and combined their metal trade with work on their small-holding. In Wigan, craft gilds controlled the production of pewter-ware and brass-ware, but normally the metal industries were organised by masters in much the same way as clothiers organised the textile industry. The masters were often craftsmen themselves, but when their businesses developed, as they frequently did in the eighteenth century, they found that organising left them no time for work at the forge or the bench.

The Industrial Revolution called for metal work on a much bigger scale than the cottage forge could produce. Fortunately, improvements to the Abraham Darby coke-smelting process, coupled with steam-engine power, made it possible for men with money to employ labour to produce larger pieces of malleable iron. Tool-making and clock-making skills, which were traditional in many Lancashire families, were turned into machinery-making skills, and from 1770 to 1870 the demand first for textile machinery and bigger steam-engines and then for locomotives, railway lines and iron ships created an ever-widening market. During the last thirty years of the eighteenth century, several textile-machinery makers established themselves in Manchester, Salford, Blackburn, Bolton, and Rochdale. In 1787 a blast furnace was built at Haigh, and within four or five years a large iron foundry was working in Salford. Before 1800 the engineering firm of Bateman and Sherratt of Salford was employing hundreds of workmen, and about 1800 Peel, Williams and Company in Ancoats, Manchester, began to make such special items as gears, shafting, and presses as well as steam-engines. Before long James Nasmyth was experimenting with mass-production methods at his Patricroft works, and by 1832 the Vulcan factory at Earlestown, as well as the older established Fairbairn's of Manchester, had begun making locomotives.

Copper-smelting and the production of copper goods was another important metal industry active in eighteenth- and nineteenth-century Lancashire. Thomas Patten opened his Bank Quay copper works in Warrington in 1717. His son, another Thomas, extended the business beyond all expectation. Before 1800, however, the industry moved to St. Helens, where coal was cheaper. Most ore then came from Anglesey, and, thanks to the Sankey Canal, it could be carried to St. Helens just as conveniently as to Warrington.

Copper-smelting still continued at St. Helens at the beginning of this present century, but for many decades it had been overshadowed there by the glass industry. In 1773 John Mackay and Company built a casting-hall at Ravenhead, St. Helens, to manufacture plate glass. There were earlier 'glass-houses' than this in Liverpool, Warrington, Bickerstaffe, and Thatto Heath, now part of St. Helens, but Mackay's factory was the beginning of large-scale manufacture in Lancashire. Thanks to such successors as the United Glass Bottle Company and Pilkington Brothers with their subsidiaries Triplex and Fibreglass, St. Helens has long been the glass capital of Britain.

Top o' th' Coal Pits, Blackburn, by Charles Haworth, 1816-95. The circular structure is a horse-gin or whim, used to wind up the coal from the pit about 250 feet deep

XX Salt Refining and the Chemical Industry

Pack horses

About 1790 John Holt wrote that no other 'article of Commerce' had contributed more 'to the present flourishing state of the Town of Liverpool' than the salt trade. He was looking back at the steady development of the trade over a full hundred years, ever since rock salt had first been mined near Northwich at the end of the seventeenth century. Before that time the output of the Cheshire brine pits had been limited by the double expense of carrying coal by pack-horse and barge from Prescot to the salt field, and of bringing back the refined salt as far as Frodsham Bridge before it could be loaded into barges and sailed to Liverpool. So heavy were transport charges that coal, which cost three shillings a ton at the pithead in Prescot, could not be delivered at Northwich for much less than four times that sum. But rock salt could be carried straight from the salt mine to Lancashire, and could be refined much more cheaply at sites on the edge of the coal field. Within three or four years of the beginning of rock-salt mining, new refineries had been built at Frodsham, Liverpool and Dungeon, near Hale. The Weaver Navigation project in the 'twenties of the eighteenth century, followed by the cutting of the Sankey Canal in the 'fifties, substantially reduced the cost of carrying both salt and coal. The rock-salt industry progressed steadily, and cheaper transport enabled the brine industry to recover and compete again in price. By 1760 20,000 tons of refined salt were being brought down the Weaver to Liverpool every year, but before the end of the century the annual tonnage was more than five times as big. So valuable was the trade that Liverpool merchants such as Joseph Leigh and Nicholas Ashton sought to control it completely by purchasing brine pits in Cheshire and coal mines near St. Helens. By 1830 the salt industry had almost become a monopoly in the hands of a few Liverpool men.

The demand for salt never slackened. Apart from its universal use as a condiment, it was used in considerable quantities for preserving meat and fish, for curing hides and skins, for glazing pottery, and even as a fertiliser for certain crops such as sugar beet and mangolds. Livepool ships carried salt to other parts of Britain, to Ireland, to the Baltic and the Mediterranean, to Newfoundland, and to the West Indies and the American colonies. Cheshire salt successfully challenged the reputation and sale of French salt, which had enjoyed pre-eminence in the seventeenth century. Moreover, the ships which carried the

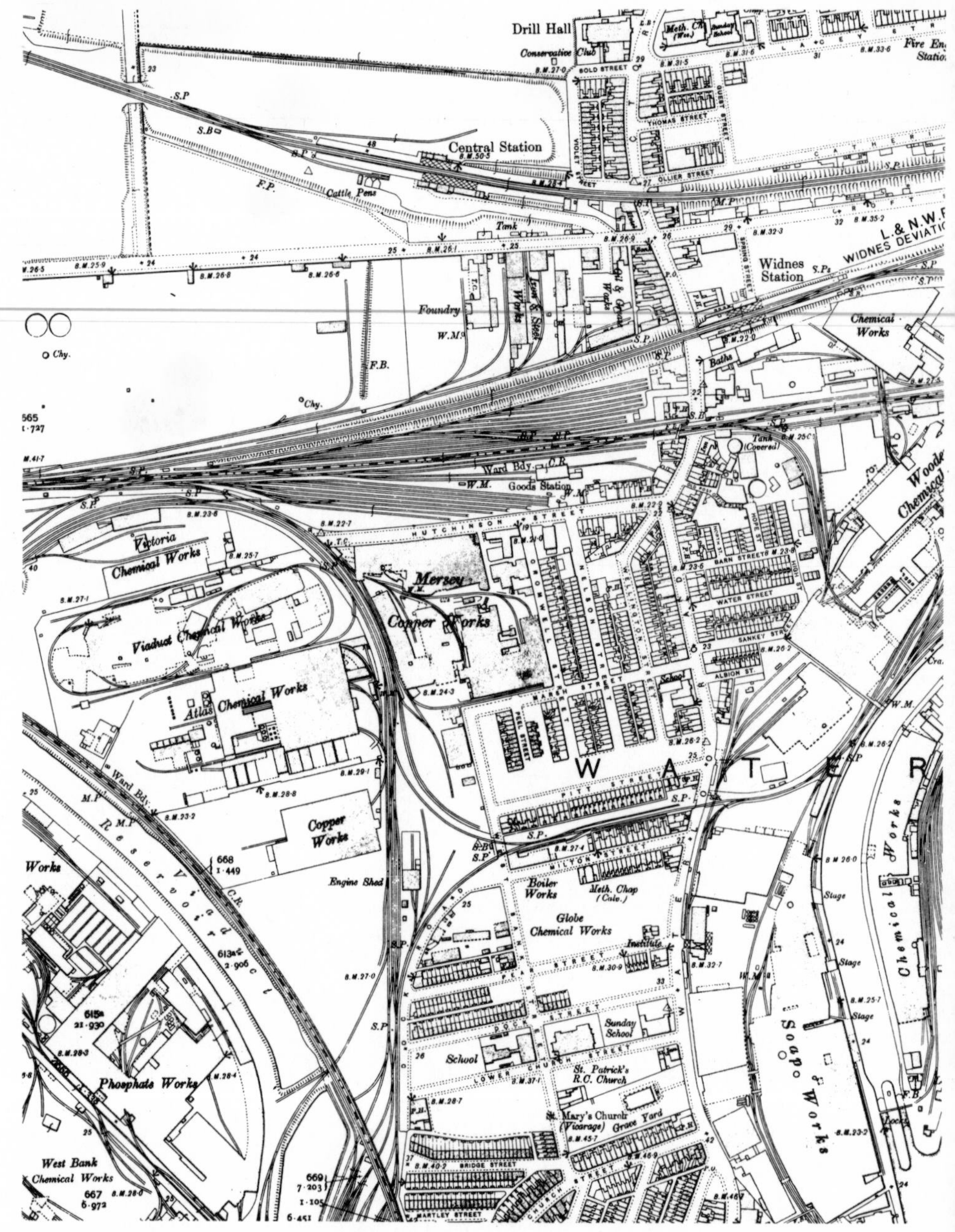

Part of Industrial Widnes, *c.* 1895

The Sankey Canal, in the right bottom corner of this map, reached Widnes in 1830, but almost all the industrial development of the town dates from *c.* 1850. The map shows how rapidly it grew.

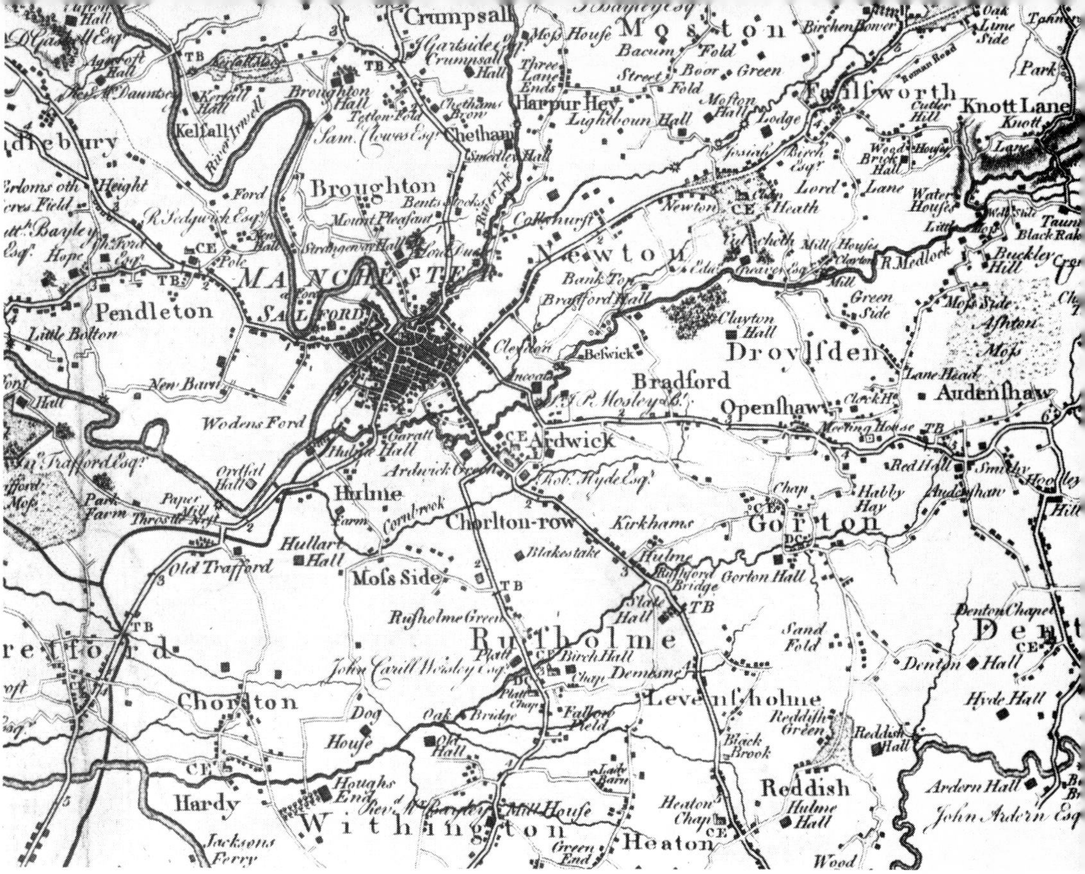

33 and 34. Two sections of Yates's Map of Lancashire, 1787. Double lines indicate turnpike roads, single lines canals. T.B. = toll-bar; R. = rectory; V. = vicarage, C.E. = chapel of ease D.C. = dissenters' chapel.

35. The Old Dock, Liverpool, completed 1719, abandoned and filled in 1825.

36. Prince's Dock, Liverpool, opened 1821.

salt away from Liverpool brought back valuable cargoes, some of which, like China clay from Cornwall and timber from Scandinavia, themselves established or expanded Merseyside industries. Indeed towards the end of the eighteenth century Merseyside itself began to use increasing quantities of salt, since potteries, tanneries, soapworks and glassworks recently established in south-west Lancashire all needed salt as a raw material. Soap making on Merseyside developed exceptionally quickly, and had become a valuable export trade by 1830. Salt was also required by the chemical works which were established at Liverpool, St. Helens, and Newton to supply soapworks with soda ash for making caustic soda, and the textile industry with the sulphuric acid and chlorine which it required in increasing quantities for its bleaching processes. The opening of new salt fields at Winsford about 1800 and the coming of rail transport thirty years later helped the salt industry to keep pace with the ever-increasing demand. In 1840 Cheshire produced half a million tons of salt: by 1870 the annual production had reached a million tons.

A Liverpool Pottery

Not until the middle of the nineteenth century did the chemical industry begin to centre upon Widnes. The Leblanc process of producing alkalis required salt, limestone, vitriol and coal, and Widnes, situated at the Mersey end of the extended Sankey Canal, was in a good position to obtain these commodities cheaply. Coal was the most expensive item in the process, and the canal and the Widnes–St. Helens railway ensured adequate supplies at reasonable prices. John Hutchinson from St. Helens, James Muspratt from Liverpool, and William Gossage from Worcestershire, especially realised the industrial possibilities of Widnes. Between 1847 and 1855 the first seven chemical works were built there, and it was not long before others followed. After 1865 new processes were introduced to extract chlorine from the hydrochloric-acid gas with which the Leblanc process polluted the atmosphere, and sulphur from the waste. Glycerine was made from soap lees. The town grew rapidly and by 1880 Widnes chemical works were employing about 10,000 workmen. But already the position which Widnes had so quickly established was being challenged. Brunner, Hutchinson's office manager, and Mond, a German chemist, had bought from Belgium the rights of producing alkali by the new Solvay or ammonia-soda process, and despite their initial difficulties in establishing their new works at Winnington in Cheshire, and despite the Widnes manufacturers' attempts to produce more cheaply, the days of the Leblanc process were numbered. In 1890 the Leblanc manufacturers formed the United Alkali Company to reorganise the industry, but the advantages of amalgamation were offset by fresh competition from the Castner-Keller factory which was set up at Weston Point,

Runcorn in 1897. Castner-Kellner's manufactured chlorine and caustic soda from brine by electrolysis, and with their up-to-date plant undercut the United Alkali Company's prices.

The war with Germany which began in 1914 so increased the demand for chemicals, that the government was prepared to help with money and materials to increase the efficiency of the industry. The last traces of the Leblanc process disappeared, for the United Alkali Company adopted electrolytic methods. After the war a number of industries subsidiary to the main chemical industry, such as the manufacture of fertilisers and flavouring essences, came to Widnes, but on the other hand Gossage's soap works was closed down in 1931. The industrial slump of that period caused Lever Brothers, who had taken over Gossage's after the war, to decide that all soap manufacture in south Lancashire should be concentrated in Warrington. The organisation of the chemical industry was fundamentally reformed in 1926 when the leading chemical firms, including old rivals such as the United Alkali Company, Brunner-Mond's and Castner-Kellner's, merged to form Imperial Chemical Industries. The new organisation kept its research laboratory in Widnes, but it moved the headquarters of its General Division to Liverpool, and of its Salt Division to Winnington. The Widnes works now use Cheshire brine, which is pumped through a pipeline carried across the Mersey by the railway bridge, and they still manufacture large quantities of chlorine, caustic soda, and sulphuric acid.

Though the days have gone when chemical fumes turned household brasses in Widnes and St. Helens green and blue within hours of being cleaned, the chemical industry has bequeathed ugly waste-heaps to south Lancashire. Some of this waste is now being used as a fertiliser, and land made derelict by nineteenth-century industry is being steadily reclaimed.

XXI Parliamentary Representation in Lancashire

The distribution of parliamentary seats and the qualifications for voters had remained virtually unchanged for four hundred years before the Whig government under Lord Grey passed the Great Reform Act of 1832. To make matters worse those four hundred years included the years of the Industrial Revolution with their major population movements and the development of industrial towns. The census of 1801 gave the population of Lancashire as 673,486. The county's fourteen members of Parliament, the same number that had represented it in the Tudor parliaments, needed to be both doubled, and drastically redistributed, to give the county adequate representation. By 1831, when the census return was 1,336,854, the position had become ludicrous. Orator Hunt, the Radical M.P. for Preston, pointed out in the Commons that all that Lord John Russell had said when he introduced the Reform Bill in 1831 'had been said twenty years ago by the weavers of Lancashire'. He himself had argued the case for Parliamentary Reform hundreds of times, including the ill-starred occasion of Peterloo, when in 1819 nervous magistrates, fearing wide-scale disturbances, had ordered a detachment of yeomanry to charge into and disperse the large crowd, which had assembled in St. Peter's Fields, Manchester, to hear him speak. A dozen people had been killed and hundreds injured. This disaster made the reformers in Lancashire more determined than ever to agitate for reform. They saw no reason why Manchester, Bolton, Blackburn, Oldham and other growing towns should continue to be unrepresented in Parliament; or why voters in Liverpool, Lancaster and Wigan should be limited to a minority of 'freemen', or voters in the county area to 'forty-shilling freeholders'. The most democratic elections in Lancashire, and in Britain, took place in Preston. In 1661 the Commons had declared that 'all the inhabitants' of Preston had the right to vote, and though this right was not enforced until 'the great election' of 1768, and though *all* never included women or minors, it remained the rule in the borough until 1832. In 1830 Hunt polled 3,730 votes against Stanley's 3,392. Out of a population of 36,000 these were big figures. Newton was the least democratic of Lancashire boroughs. Its freeman status was ignored, and its M.P.s were nominated by the Legh family, the lords of the manor.

John Gladstone, father of the prime minister and leader of the Liverpool Tories in the early nineteenth century

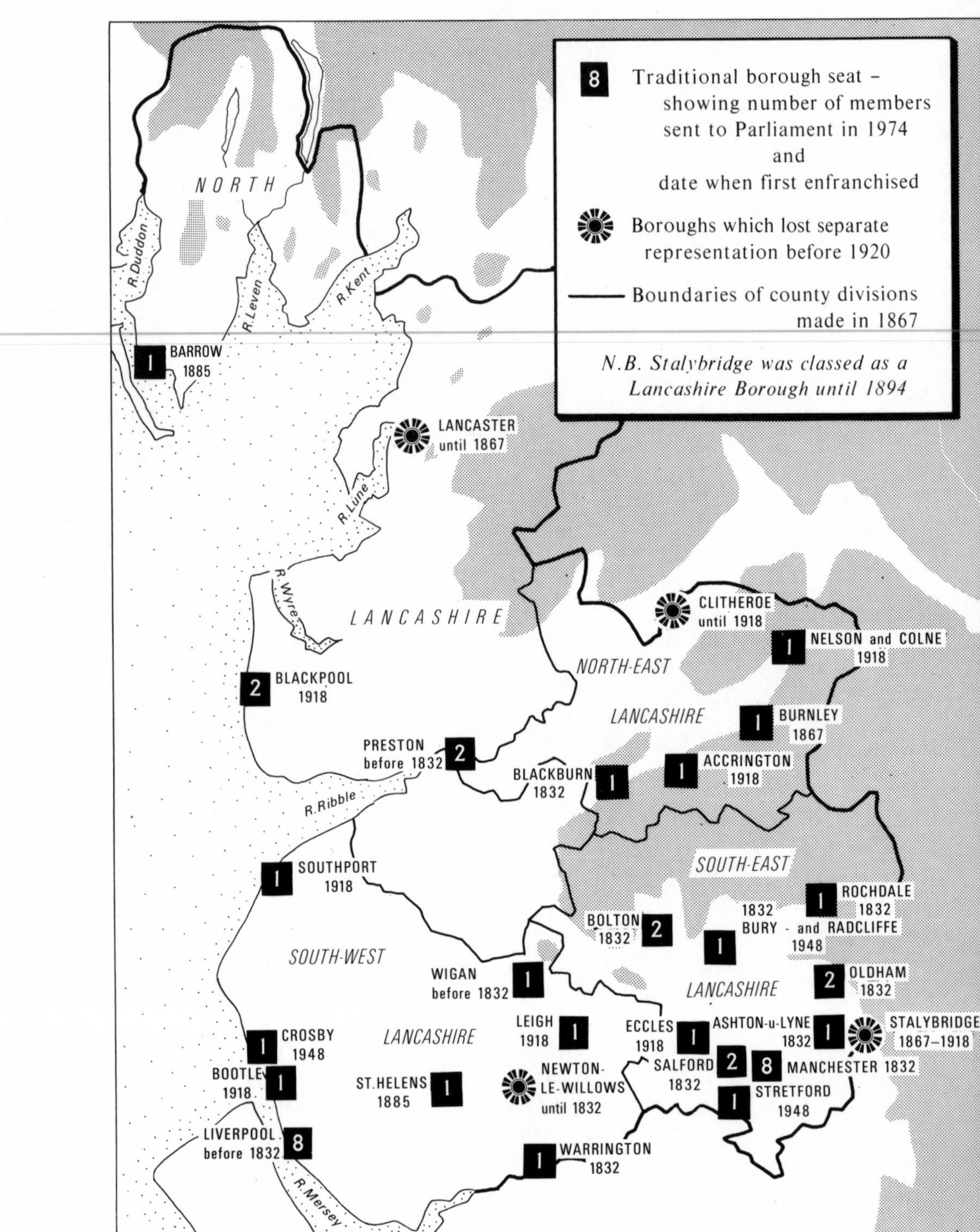

Parliamentary Representation

In spite of its name the Great Reform Act of 1832 was a mild measure. It confiscated 143 seats from 'rotten' and small boroughs, and distributed them among those unrepresented boroughs that, in the government's opinion, had the best claim. Newton lost both its seats, Clitheroe one. Two seats each were given to Manchester, Oldham, Bolton, and Blackburn, and one seat each to Ashton-under-Lyne, Bury, Rochdale, Salford, and Warrington. In addition the county area was divided into two constituencies, North Lancashire and South Lancashire, each with two representatives. The county franchise was widened, and in the boroughs, much to the disappointment of thousands of working-class 'reformers', the vote was restricted to '£10 householders'. Lancashire had now twenty-six M.P.s, but its representation was still inadequate for the size of its population.

E. G. Stanley, M.P. for Preston 1826-30, for North Lancs. 1833-44. As earl of Derby (1851-69) three times prime minister

Many discontented Radicals joined the Chartist Movement, which from 1838 to 1848 advocated further reforms, including equal electoral districts, secret ballot and the right to vote for every man over twenty-one. Feargus O'Connor, the northern leader of the movement, gained most of his support in Lancashire from the textile towns.

In 1861 South Lancashire was given a third member, and by the Reform Act of 1867, which enfranchised all householders in the boroughs, Burnley and Stalybridge were each given a seat for the first time, an extra member was given to Liverpool, Manchester, and Salford, and the county was divided into four divisions each of which had two members. On the other hand the act disfranchised Lancaster. The Redistribution Act which accompanied Gladstone's Reform Act of 1884 further increased Lancashire representation, and it divided into single-member constituencies both the county area and those boroughs which had more than two representatives. Since then there have been periodic redistribution acts, and in the 1974 election Lancashire sent to Parliament some sixty members. Traditionally M.P.s were divided into county members and borough members. That division became increasingly unreal. Crosby and Leigh, for example, were classed as *boroughs,* but Farnworth and Chorley were *county constituencies.* By the 1960s the distinction was being ignored, and the local government changes of 1974 made it meaningless.

The 1918 Reform Act changed the voting qualification from 'all householders' to men over twenty-one years and women over thirty. Ten years later Parliament abolished the distinction between men's and women's qualifications.

Lancashire had its fair share of electoral corruption before the Secret Ballot Act of 1872 made it pointless as well as illegal to try and gain votes by offering bribes to, or by threatening reprisals against, the electors. As late as 1868, the Liberals in the South-West Lancashire constituency reckoned that each vote cast for their candidates, W. E. Gladstone and H. R. Grenfell, cost £1 2s. 0d. Yet Gladstone had forbidden all bribery, and such enthusiastic supporters as Lord Sefton and Lady Scarisbrick had promised to 'persuade' their tenants to vote Liberal. Earlier elections were far more expensive than this one. Freemen in the boroughs traditionally regarded their vote as saleable. They took it for granted that they would enjoy unlimited food and drink during the election week or fortnight, but most of them, middle-class as well as artisan, looked for a money payment as well. In the Liverpool election of 1812, for example, it cost the supporters of George Canning at least £18,000 to gain his winning 1,631 votes. In the notorious 1830 by-election, when, in Henry Brougham's words, 'corruption walked forth in open day and huckstered at the foot of the hustings', the costs of the successful William Ewart reached a staggering £65,000. The Commons considered this outrageous and declared this Liverpool election void. They did the same after the 1866 Lancaster election, when it was shown that E. W. Fenwick and H. W. Schneider had bribed their way to success. Indeed, in the following year, chronic corruption was one of the main arguments for disfranchising the borough of Lancaster.

Tory Election Cartoon, Liverpool Election, 1818

XXII Lancashire and the Corn Laws

William Huskisson M.P. for Liverpool 1823-30

The Corn Laws of 1815 forbade the import of foreign corn until home-grown corn had reached the famine price of 80s. a quarter. Most support for this drastic measure came from two groups—those who still held the outdated mercantilist belief that Britain's wealth consisted of the gold she accumulated by constantly exporting more goods than she imported, and those who, more basely, feared a fall in agricultural rents if corn did not continue to command the high prices of the war years. Opposition was slow to develop, although dear bread and low wages were creating obvious hardships for factory and agricultural workers, and although Adam Smith's *Wealth of Nations* had been demonstrating the folly of mercantilist thinking for a full forty years. Gradually, however, the conviction grew that expanding trade was the key to national wealth, and that to curb trade by such measures as the Corn Laws was to benefit a minority at the expense of the majority.

Yet neither Whigs nor Tories were prepared to repeal the Corn Laws. In 1828 William Huskisson, Tory M.P. for Liverpool and President of the Board of Trade, modified their effect with his sliding scale. This placed an import duty on foreign corn, high when home-grown wheat fell in price, and low when it was dear. Before the 1841 election, the Tories promised to make the scale more favourable to the consumer, and the Whigs advocated a fixed duty of 8s. a quarter. Abolitionists, therefore, had to crusade on their own. The trade depression and bad harvests of 1837-42 played into their hands.

In September 1838 a small group of Lancashire merchants met in the *York Hotel,* King Street, Manchester to found the Anti-Corn-Law Association. For the next eight years the League, as the Association was soon re-named, conducted a vigorous national campaign. Unlike the contemporary Chartist Movement with which it competed for support in the factory towns, the League had a single, clearly-understood aim—the abolition of the Corn Laws. It hammered its message home incessantly. From the first, cotton manufacturers gave it adequate funds, and it soon discovered two effective orators and administrators in Richard Cobden, a Manchester calico manufacturer, and John Bright, a Rochdale millowner. Its public meetings ranged from street-corner gatherings, frequently addressed by paid agitators, and sometimes provoking violence, to well-advertised, well-attended, socially-respectable rallies in large public halls. Cobden's unending argument was that Britain could buy Europe's surplus corn with increased cotton exports. 'What we desire is plenty of corn. . . . To pay for it more manufactures would be required from this country; this would lead to an increased demand for labour in the manufacturing districts, which would necessarily be attended with a rise of wages'. Bright stressed the social injustice of the bread-tax and maintained with Cobden that experience showed that 'whenever corn has been cheap, wages have been high in Lancashire; and, on the other hand, when bread has been dear, wages have been greatly reduced . . .'.

Cobden's House in Quay Street, Manchester

In Peter Street, Manchester, in January 1840, a wooden hall, appropriately named the Free Trade Hall, was erected in less than a fortnight to accommodate Anti-Corn-Law audiences. Three years later, a capacious brick hall took its place, and in 1856, a decade after the League's triumph, this in turn was replaced by the handsome stone building which is illustrated opposite page 65.

The League kept its cause alive and stimulated public agitation by frequent campaigns, processions, effigy-burnings and monster meetings. It used the new penny post to drop pamphlets on the nation's breakfast table, and the new railways to take its speakers from gathering to gathering and to distribute its propaganda and its newspaper, *The League*. But clearly, the final victory could only be won at Westminster. In 1841 Stockport elected Cobden its M.P., and two years later, Bright won a bye-election in Durham. With the help of Charles Villiers, member for Wolverhampton, the two of them led a nagging, relentless attack upon the Tory government's refusal to repeal the Corn Laws. Sir Robert Peel, the Prime Minister, who came from Bury where his father had built a large cotton-printing works, was not unsympathetic to free trade principles. Indeed, in 1842 and 1845, his government abolished or reduced duties on many imports, but for at least two reasons he was not prepared to repeal the Corn Laws. He held that in time of war it would be dangerous for Britain to be dependent on imported corn—the submarine blockade during the 1914–18 war later demonstrated the strength of that argument—and he knew that many of his supporters, especially in the Lords, believed that their personal well-being depended upon tariffs continuing to protect English corn-growing.

Cobden's and Bright's arguments converted Peel even before the Irish potato famine compelled him, in June 1846, to split his party and ruin his own political future by repealing the Corn Laws. Industrial Lancashire was delighted. The League had triumphed unexpectedly quickly and had no further reason to exist. Masters and men saw palmy days ahead for cotton, and expressed their joy with a public holiday and gay processions. Manchester made a brave show. Bands from Stockport and Rochdale marched through its streets with lamp-lighters, tradesmen and civic dignitaries from Manchester and Salford. On that summer's day it seemed no boast to claim that what Manchester thinks today London will think tomorrow.

Sir Robert Peel born at Bury, 1778

Cobden had devoted so much time and energy to the League's campaign, that by 1846 his neglected calico business lay in ruins. Fortunately a grateful public presented him with a testimonial of more than £60,000. This saved him from bankruptcy, and enabled him to continue campaigning for the abolition of the remaining restrictions on British trade. In 1859-60, he negotiated a difficult commercial treaty between England and France. To this achievement, Gladstone, born in Liverpool and M.P. for South Lancashire from 1865 to 1868, paid worthy, if pompous, tribute: 'Rare is the privilege of any man, who, having fourteen years ago rendered to his country one signal and splendid service, now again with the same brief span of life, decorated neither by rank nor title, bearing no mark to distinguish him from the people whom he serves, has been permitted to perform a great and memorable service to his country'. Cobden died in 1865, but, especially in Lancashire, his name continued to be associated with free trade. *Manchester School* became the accepted title of the most ardent group of free trade politicians, and most cotton towns built a Cobden Club during the next few years.

John Bright, seven years Cobden's junior, was only in his middle thirties in 1846. Manchester returned him as its member in 1847 and 1852, and since his political interests were not as specialised as Cobden's he worked for many different causes. He enthusiastically supported the extension of the franchise, the admission of Jews into Parliament and the transference of the powers of the East India Company to the Government, and he led opposition to the Crimean War, to Palmerston's expansionist policy in China and, in 1882, to Gladstone's 'aggression' in Egypt. From the mid-'sixties he called himself a Liberal, but his Quaker principles and his tender conscience made him a poor party politician. He remained an outstanding individualist, as resounding an orator as Gladstone, and a personality who won the respect of his political opponents.

XXIII *The Development of the Lancashire Coast*

'Southport' in the 1780s. Yates's Map

Sea bathing became increasingly fashionable in the eighteenth century. By 1721 wooden bathing huts graced the shore at Liverpool. A generation later Blackpool was letting its first bathing 'accommodations', and soon after that, visitors to North Meols were regularly travelling two miles to the south 'in carts and other conveyances which could be procured, on account of its being much better bathing'. There at South Hawes, the enterprising William Sutton of North Meols built the *South Port Hotel* for seabathers. This *folly,* as his neighbours dubbed it, Sutton first occupied in 1798. It was the beginning of present-day Southport.

In 1788 William Hutton of Birmingham took his family on holiday to Blackpool. He stayed for three months at the *Lane Ends Hotel,* situated at the junction of the present Church Street and Promenade. According to a 'to let' notice of the previous year, *Lane Ends,* one of Blackpool's four hotels, had 70 beds, 'necessary and proper furniture' and adequate stabling. Hutton's daughter, Catherine, described the patrons as 'rich, rough, honest manufacturers of the town of Bolton': she considered that the other hotels, *Bailey's, Forshaw's* and *Hull's,* had more genteel company, 'Lancashire gentry, Liverpool merchants and Manchester manufacturers'. Hutton thought Blackpool an excellent bathing place: 'the sea . . . retreats nearly half a mile at low water leaving a bed of most beautiful and solid sand . . .'. High-tide bathing was carefully regulated. 'A bell rings . . . as a signal for the ladies. Some use machines drawn by one horse, a few travel from their apartments in their waterdress but the majority clothe in the boxes which stand on the beach for their use. If a gentleman is seen upon the parade he forfeits a bottle of wine. When the ladies retire the bell rings for the gentlemen'.

Ellen Weeton would have approved such decorum. Over many years she enjoyed Southport's 'fine open sea' and 'spacious shore', and in 1809 felt flattered that there she shared her pleasure with 'many people of some consequence and fashion'. But by 1825 she found the resort 'sadly exposing'. Gentlemen's and ladies' bathing machines were 'standing promiscuously in the water', and 'at spring tides it is hardly possible to have a machine for only one person, such crowds resort there to bathe'. That very season the lords of the manor, Hesketh and Bold, put an end to such frivolity. They marked out the shore with posts, and ordered their stewards to ensure that at least one hundred yards of 'vacant space' separated men and women bathers.

About this time, too, Morecambe Bay was attracting more visitors. Sunderland was said to be a place 'much resorted for sea bathing'. The hotel at Heysham advertised 'excellent baths and bathing machines', and the *Lancaster Gazette* reported that in Regatta Week, July 1829, Poulton, the future Morecambe, was 'numerously and fashionably attended'.

Horse-drawn bathing hut

Nevertheless, it was not easy to reach the Lancashire resorts. In the 1780s two or three coaches were running a thrice-weekly summer service from Manchester to Blackpool, but each carried a mere dozen passengers and charged 13s. 6d. for the single journey. By the turn of the century, a few coaches, usually one a week during the season, were taking holiday-makers to Blackpool from the bigger West Riding towns, but even after 1816, when a daily coach service first linked Preston and Blackpool, most visitors continued to arrive in their own cart or chaise, on horseback or on foot. In the 1820s summer travellers from Liverpool to Southport could either ride in *The Eclipse,* the daily coach, or sail by the canal packet as far as the *Red Lion* at Scarisbrick and then complete the journey by landau. By the early 1830s *The Royal Sailor* provided a regular coach service between Morecambe and Lancaster, to which centre for many years canal packets had been conveying visitors from both Preston and Kendal. Yet neither canal packets nor horse-drawn coaches were capable of bringing large holiday crowds to the seaside. It needed the capacity, speed and cheapness of the railway train to do that.

The Preston–Fleetwood railway opened in July 1840 and was extended from Poulton-le-Fylde to Blackpool in April 1846. Blackpool quickly felt the effect, and during the next generation the well-known features of the resort steadily appeared—the north and central piers in the 'seventies, the electric tramway in the 'eighties, and the tower and south pier in the 'nineties. Morecambe's growth was not quite so spectacular, but from 1848, when trains began a shuttle service to Lancaster, the resort had steadily to build more hotels and boarding-houses to accommodate its visitors.

The resort which at first grew most rapidly, however, was Southport, the one nearest to the industrial towns. Once the railway had joined it to Liverpool in 1850 and to Manchester in 1855, it developed both as a holiday centre and as a dormitory for middle-class city workers. During Whit week 1855, 40,000 visitors arrived by rail from Manchester and the cotton towns. More significantly still, scores of 'in-comelings' began to build homes in Southport and neighbouring Birkdale. The 1871 census gave the combined permanent population of Southport and Birkdale as 21,451 against Blackpool's 6,100 and Morecambe's (together with Bare and Torrisholme) 3,005. Already, in 1867, Southport had been incorporated as a borough, a distinction not achieved by Blackpool until 1876 and by Morecambe until 1902.

The petrol engine has brought these resorts and many lesser ones within much easier reach of industrial centres. In each decade of this century more people have visited the coast and more people have built homes there.

Gathering cockles and mussels in Morecambe Bay in the nineteenth century.

XXIV *Lancashire's Industrial Towns—their Growth and Public Health Problem*

Oldham in 1780s. Yates's map

In the nineteenth century the population of England Wales quadrupled. Most Lancashire towns and villages north of the Ribble grew no faster than towns and villages in other counties. But south of the Ribble and in a few isolated places to the north, maps and censuses show a dramatic growth of urban areas. The older centres of trade and communications expanded until they were at least five times as big: the 1801 and 1901 census figures, for example, for Warrington are 10,567 and 56,892, for Wigan 10,989 and 60,764, and for Preston 11,887 and 101,295. But in textile Lancashire there was not only a big overall increase of population but also a marked concentration of people into industrial centres in the lower, wider valleys. Before this process began, not one of the textile towns, with the outstanding exception of Manchester, was much bigger than a village. The industry, based partly on the cottage worker and partly on water-wheel machinery (see pages 84-6), was scattered over many small townships, so that as Yates's map shows, there was little difference in size between parish centres, such as Rochdale or Ashton-under-Lyne, and neighbouring chapelries or townships, such as Wardle and Butterworth or Droylsden and Failsworth. The ruins of isolated farms and cottages on the hillsides and the abandoned sites of water-driven mills in many a Pennine valley are archaeological evidence of the far-reaching social and industrial changes which began and progressed in East Lancashire during George III's reign. Sheep farming on a modest scale ceased to be possible once the farmer could no longer depend upon supplementing his meagre profits with family earnings from domestic spinning and weaving, and the reliability of the steam-engine made it possible for millowners to move from the inconvenient upper valleys and build their new mills where communications and house-building were much easier.

Oldham is one of several such villages which galloped to borough status in the nineteenth century. Yates's map shows its progress beginning with a mile of ribbon development along the Huddersfield road. By 1801 it had achieved a population of 12,024. Fifty years later it had grown to 52,820, and by 1901 to 137,246. Baines's *Directory* of 1825 explained why this spinning town was growing so fast: 'Sixty years ago there was not a cotton mill on the chapelry; at present there

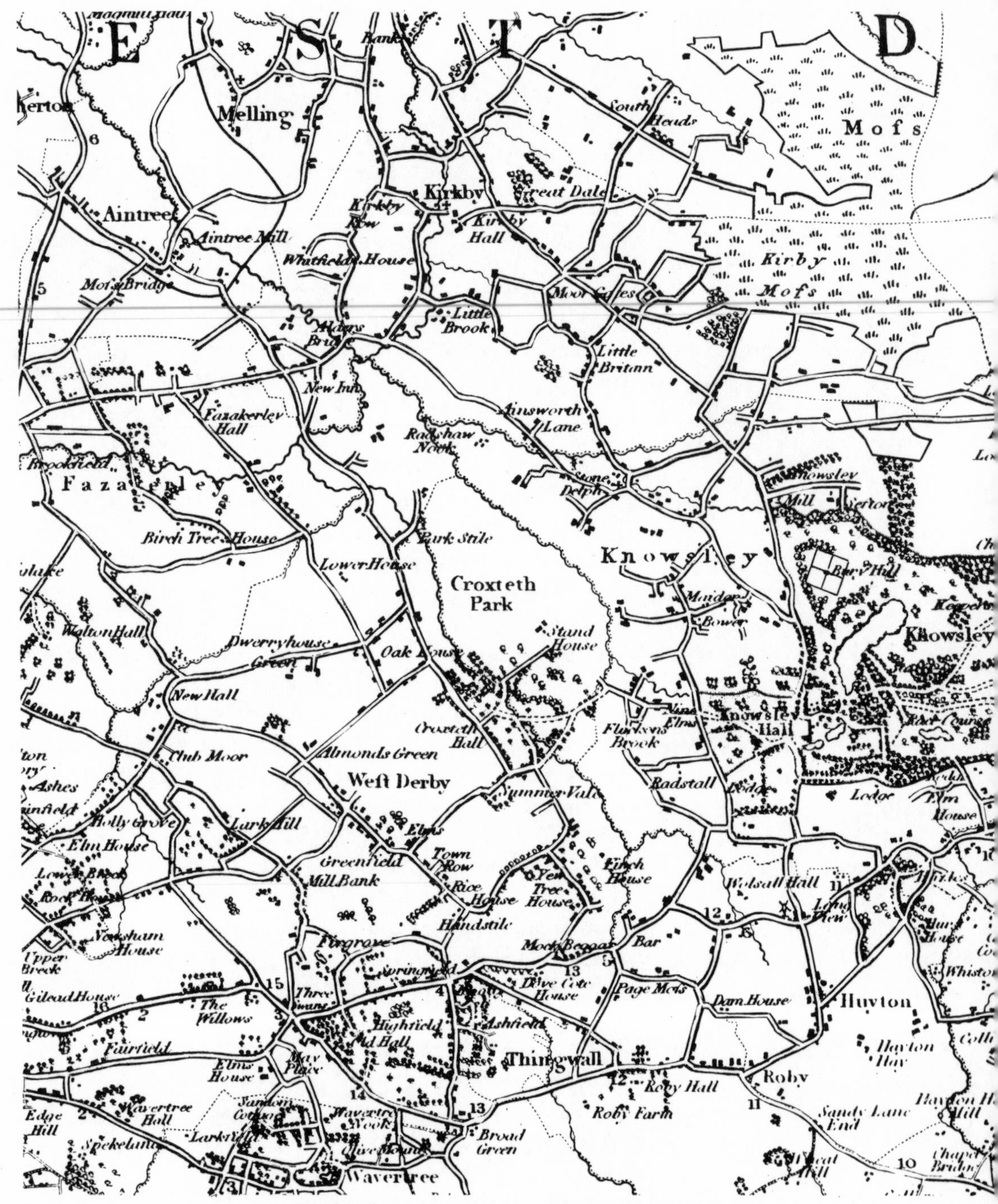

Part of Greenwood's Map of Lancashire, 1818

This country area to the east and north-east of Liverpool is now largely covered with the city's housing estates and suburban dwellings.

are no fewer than sixty-five . . . which are wholly employed in spinning cotton and are all worked by steam'. Outbursts of industrial prosperity caused Oldham's mills to go on expanding until the 1914–18 war. Blackburn is a weaving town with a similar history. Despite its prestige as the centre of a hundred and of a large, medieval parish, its population in 1780 was no more than 5,000. Then, as Oldham did, it began to grow, especially after the advent of the steam-driven loom. By 1801 its population had more than doubled–11,980. By 1851 it had reached 46,536, and by the turn of the century 108,865.

Blackburn Parish Church. Drawn by S. J. Allan, 1820

A number of non-textile Lancashire towns have much the same sort of life story. The 'flashes' and the slag heaps on the coalfields are today's reminders of nineteenth-century improvements, which replaced the hundreds of separate, shallow coal-pits shown on Yates's map with fewer, larger mines tapping the richer deep seams. This industrial change caused a concentration of colliers in towns such as Wigan and Worsley, or in colliery villages such as Billinge and Tyldesley. The siting of glass and copper industries on the coalfield steadily transformed a cross-roads, chapel and inn on Yates's map into the centre of modern St. Helens, and later, railway transport made possible the building of Widnes and Barrow on virtually virgin sites.

But the two boom towns of nineteenth-century Lancashire were undoubtedly Manchester and Liverpool. From at least the sixteenth century, Manchester had been the largest town in Lancashire. At the time of the Civil Wars, it had a population of about 5,000; when the Young Pretender marched through, about 17,000; and in 1801, just over 70,000. In 1838, the year the townships of Manchester, Cheetham, Hulme, Ardwick, Chorlton-on-Medlock and Beswick were incorporated into a borough, the combined population was given as 242,357. Thenceforward the borough–and from 1853 the city–grew rapidly both in area and in population. It passed the half-million mark in the late 1890s, and reached the highest figure of all–over 750,000– at the 1931 census. Manchester owes its size and importance largely to the development of the cotton trade, but also to coalmining, engineering and the network of roads, canals and railways which radiate from it. It is the natural social, administrative and commercial centre for densely-populated south-east Lancashire.

Liverpool's growth was slightly more rapid than Manchester's. Census figures for 1801, 1851, and 1901 are 77,653, 376,065, and 684,947 respectively. In 1835 it absorbed Kirkdale, Everton and the nearer halves of Toxteth Park and West Derby, and sixty years later Walton, Wavertree and the remainder of Toxteth and West Derby. In 1868 Bootle became a separate borough.

Nineteenth-century Blackburn

Since the first world war, the population of several textile towns has decreased, but other industrial towns have continued to grow. Manchester and Liverpool particularly have built extensive new housing estates on their perimeters. During the last twenty years the village of Skelmersdale has been transformed into a modern industrial town, and a second new town, based on Preston, Leyland, and Chorley, has already begun to bestride the M6 and M61 motorways.

The rapid growth of Lancashire's industrial towns created lasting housing problems. Except in periodic spells of trade depression, the new mills, coal mines, factories and docks were greedy for labour. And since cheap public transport did not yet exist, skilled and unskilled workers alike had to live within walking distance of their work.

In Liverpool and Manchester, hundreds of poor families crowded into the town houses which the well-to-do had abandoned in order to commute in their carriages to such early suburbs as Everton and Fallowfield. Crofts and gardens in the town centres were transformed into cramped courts, and cellars were accepted as normal working-class homes. As early as 1801 Liverpool had 2,300 people living in cellars: by 1846 this figure had reached 40,000, and during the next two years a further 80,000 Irish refugees were seeking space to eat and sleep in the teeming alleys and courts behind the docks. Central Manchester was no better. In 1832 Dr. J. P. Kay described its 'mass of buildings . . . intersected by narrow and loathsome streets and close courts defiled with refuse'. The cellars, he reported, consisted 'of two rooms on a floor, each nine or ten feet square, some inhabited by ten persons, others by more'. In 1844 Friedrich Engels, the Manchester friend of Karl Marx, painted an equally sordid picture: '. . . a multitude of covered passages lead from the main street into numerous courts, and he who turns in thither gets into a filth and disgusting grime the equal of which is not to be found'.

The smaller and the newer towns were a little better off in that they had not a large core of old property to be misused in this way. Many employers built rows of utility cottages for their workmen. Most were soundly if cheaply constructed, but all were cramped and dreary, and almost all lacked piped water and privies. Stand-pipe taps or a community well, and earth closets shared by half a dozen or more families were all too common. A Board of Health inspector's report on Bacup in 1849 drew particular attention to the complete lack of passable sanitation—'Rubble-stone privies are revolting to humanity'—and to the dependence of a large section of the town on inadequate wells and springs for domestic water. Bacup was not exceptional.

CONTRASTS

7. (*above*) The last of the summer day-light on Lake Coniston.
8. (*below*) Ravenhead, one of the oldest industrial sites in South West Lancashire.

39. South Pier, Blackpool, opened 1893, thirty years after the opening North Pier and twenty five years a Central Pier.

TWO VIEWS OF LORD STRE

ASTAL RESORTS BEFORE 1914

41. Blackpool Tower, opened in 1894. This photograph was taken before the promenade was widened by 100 feet in 1904-05. Traders then set up their stalls on the sands as soon as the tide had receded.

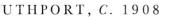

UTHPORT, *C.* 1908

43 and 44. Within two hundred yards of this bridge on tl East Lancashire road (*below*) stand the ruins of 'Windlesha Abbey' (*left*) a fifteenth-century chantry chapel found by Sir Thomas Gerard and dedicated to St. Thomas Canterbury.

Reports on Wigan, Crumpsall, Pendleton and other Lancashire towns reveal similar inadequacies.

These wretched living conditions improved but slowly, despite the frequency with which cholera, typhus and typhoid demonstrated that they could kill the rich as easily as the poor. A handful of humanitarians urged reform. A larger number of Benthamites deplored the economic loss caused by infection, chronic illness and premature death, but, as elsewhere in Victorian Britain, too many Lancastrians objected to public money being spent on social improvement. Self-help and *laissez-faire* were the popular philosophies: as *The Times* leader-writer put it, men 'refused to be bullied into health'. The authorities took some limited action. In 1844 Manchester borough council forbade the building of further back-to-back houses and laid down regulations about the construction of privies and ashpits. Two years later, Liverpool appointed Dr. W. H. Duncan public medical officer—the first, and probably the most needed, medical officer in Britain. In the middle decades of the century, Parliament authorised several Lancashire towns, which had not yet been incorporated, to elect improvement commissioners. Almost all these commissioners instituted health reforms. The St. Helens commissioners, appointed in 1845, forbade the occupation of cellars if they were not more than seven feet high and ordered the registration and inspection of lodging houses, notorious centres of disease and crime. In 1853 the Rochdale commissioners secured wider powers to improve paving and sewering. Southport's commissioners, appointed in 1846, had no acute housing problems, but they set about lighting the streets with oil naphtha lamps—although gas lighting was already the accepted method—paving the main thoroughfares with setts and laying the dust on the earth sidewalks. And Fleetwood, anxious to establish itself as a fashionable resort, threatened in 1842 to fine scavengers £5 if they did not remove dirt, ashes and rubbish, and to fine householders 5s. 0d. if they did not sweep and cleanse 'before 10 o'clock in the forenoon (Sunday excepted) the footways and pavements in front or at the side of their houses, yards and premises'. But committee resolutions did not in themselves achieve reforms. The success of each order depended upon its practicability and upon public support. Street lights or pavements were feasible, but re-housing the slum-dwellers or creating adequate sewerage required sustained effort and far more money than improvement commissioners could command. At best they only managed to make existing systems work a little more efficiently. In 1866-67 Rochdale spent on sewerage a tenth of that year's expenditure on its new town hall. During the 1860s Bolton made considerable improvements draining and paving the streets and flagging the footpaths, but out

Slum-dwellers

Entrance to Bolton's Market Hall opened in 1855

of its total expenditure of £40,500 in 1867 the town council only spent £355 on 'sanitary expenses'.

The 1848 Public Health Act permitted the central board to create a local board of health wherever a tenth of the inhabitants petitioned it to do so. Despite the obvious urgent need, only twenty-six Lancashire townships took any action at all under this act, and many of those that did petition encountered frustration and powerful opposition later. Meantime towns were growing steadily bigger and dirtier. Death rates remained appallingly high—in the early 1860s thirty-four per 1,000 in Manchester and Liverpool (47.5 and 53.4 respectively for children under fifteen years) and about twenty-seven per 1,000 in most other industrial towns. By 1865 the Manchester figure reached thirty-nine. All thinking people knew the primary causes: in 1866 one Manchester report catalogued them—'bad buildings, filthy and ill-ventilated dwellings, dark and noisome cellars, want of better draining, neglected and filthy privies, cesspools . . . vitiated atmosphere not only from smoke but various other impurities, solid, vaporous and gaseous'.

The first major step towards improved living conditions was better water supplies. Early in the nineteenth century several private water boards had built small reservoirs, occasionally in the centre of the town, to store water from local wells and rivers, but as populations increased the boards had to build much bigger reservoirs a little further afield. The Bury board went to the Ogden valley, Blackburn to Over Darwen, and Oldham to the township of Butterworth. These reservoirs, later municipally administered, still supply these towns, but neither Liverpool nor Manchester could find sufficient water locally. In the decade 1847–57, Liverpool constructed its reservoir at Rivington, but a generation later had to seek parliamentary permission to take water from Lake Vyrnwy, sixty miles away in North Wales. Manchester had a similar experience. It built its reservoirs in Longdendale on the Cheshire-Derbyshire border in the late 1840s, and by 1887 had begun the engineering work necessary to pipe water from far-away Thirlmere.

The first effective Public Health Act was passed in 1875; in the 'eighties signs of improvement began to appear. The local government reforms of 1888 and 1893 helped too, but not until after the First World War was slum clearance seriously tackled.

XXV Improved Communications, 1870s-1970s

By 1870 the railway network in Lancashire was virtually complete, and manufacturers and private travellers had become rail-minded. Already many canals were standing idle, and most turnpike trusts had either dissolved themselves already or were preparing to do so. The last to go was that responsible for the Blackburn–Preston new road in 1890. The trusts left the maintenance of their roads to the Highway District Boards established under the acts of 1862 and 1864, but after the passing of the Local Government Act of 1888 the new Lancashire County Council accepted responsibility for all main roads outside county borough boundaries. It continued to do so, either directly or as the agent for the Ministry of Transport.

Grange-over-Sands, a resort 'created' by the Furness Railway

Railway superiority led to railway monopoly. No alternative means of transport existed to keep fares and freight charges low. During the 1870s and the 1880s many Manchester cotton manufacturers and merchants were grumbling that railway charges and Liverpool dock dues were forcing them to increase their prices and reduce their profits. In 1882 they sought parliamentary permission to build an extra-wide and deep canal from the lower Mersey at Eastham to Trafford Park, so that American imports of all kinds—cotton, grain, timber and sugar—could be carried directly into the heart of Manchester. Naturally, railway shareholders, the Liverpool Cotton Association, the Liverpool steamship companies and other vested interests opposed the bill. They delayed its passing until 1885, but then, with Manchester Corporation's full support, the promoters lost little more time. Queen Victoria formally opened the Ship Canal in May 1894. It was both a noteworthy engineering achievement and a commercial success. It quickly gained its most immediate aim of reducing freight charges, and by the end of the century, with its complex of docks, wharves and warehouses, had established Manchester as the sixth busiest port in Great Britain.

With the twentieth century came the petrol engine. Steadily road transport of goods and passengers increased. In the second half of the 1920s it became necessary to build the East Lancashire Road as a new fast way between Manchester and Liverpool, and in the early 1930s to construct the Mersey Tunnel to supersede the slow, overcrowded car ferries that shuttled across the Mersey between Liverpool and Birkenhead and Seacombe. Since the end of the war in 1945 road

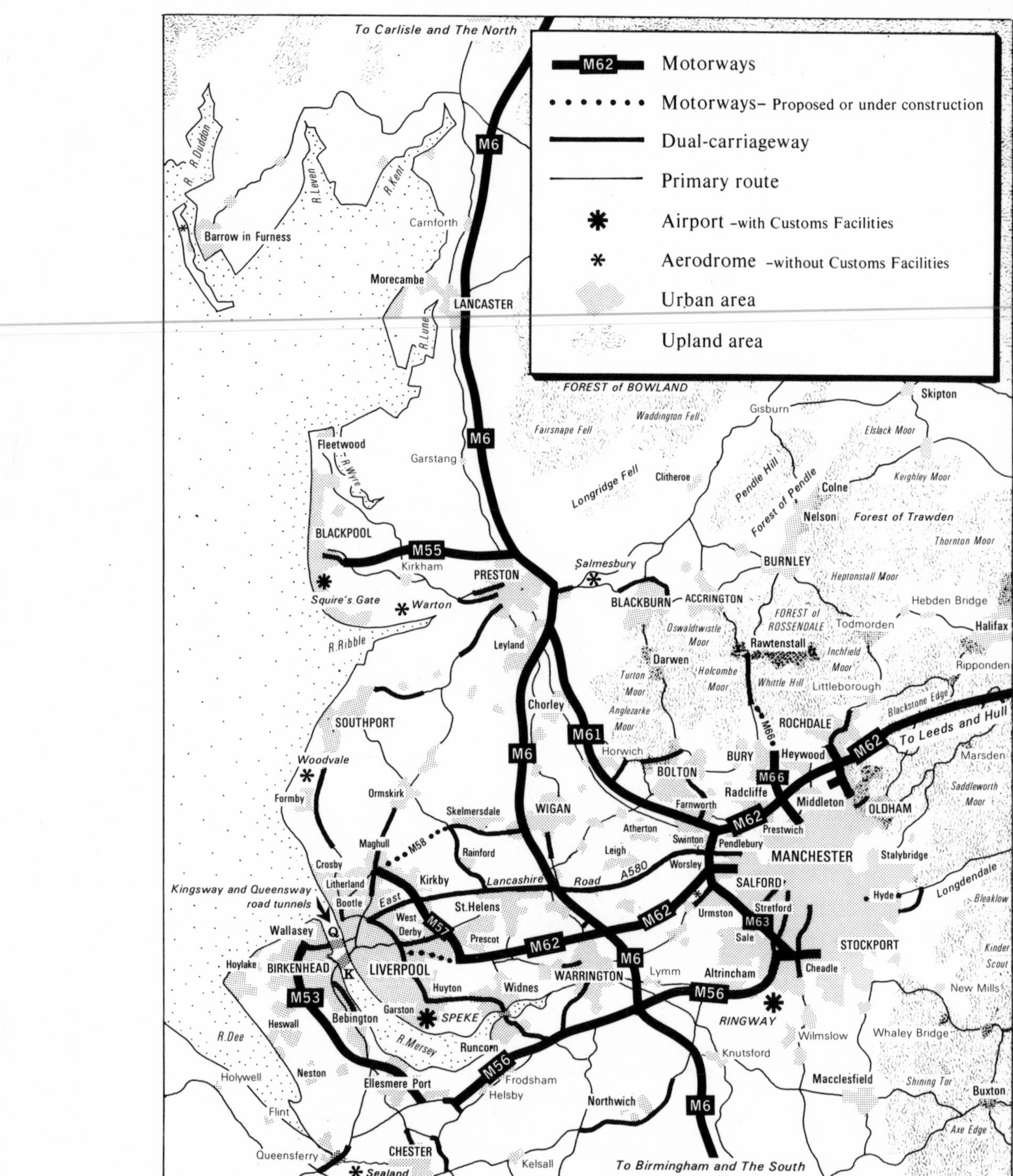

Lancashire's Motor-roads

transport has developed enormously. Existing roads and bridges have proved inadequate for the increasing load of lorries, coaches and private cars, and, in common with the rest of Britain, and indeed of the whole western world, Lancashire has had to initiate a transport revolution.

One of the air-shafts of the first Mersey tunnel

The first big task was the construction of the motorway, M6, from the south to the north of the county. This began with two stretches of by-pass, the first round Preston, opened in December 1958, and the second round Lancaster, opened in April 1960. In January 1965 it first became possible to motor from Cheshire into Lancashire across the Thelwall Viaduct, high above the Mersey and Ship Canal, and continue along the motorway almost into Westmorland. Early in the 1970s M6 not only reached Carlisle, but from Bamber Bridge was linked to Manchester by M61, and from Orrell to Skelmersdale by a wide double carriageway. In October 1960 the Stretford-Eccles by-pass was opened to provide a link between South Manchester and the East Lancashire Road. This was the first section of a network of motor-roads, which now meet at the popularly-named 'spaghetti junction', near Worsley. From this nodal point run M61 to Bamber Bridge and M63 to Cheadle; through it threads M62 on its way from Liverpool to Hull. M62 crosses M6 north of Warrington and has feeder roads from North Liverpool, Salford, and Rawtenstall. In 1975 M55 was opened to join Blackpool to M6 north of Preston.

Since 1961 a handsome high-level road bridge has replaced the old, frustrating transporter bridge between Widnes and Runcorn, so that for the first time road vehicles can readily cross the lower Mersey without going round by Warrington or through the Mersey Tunnel. On the Lancashire side of the new bridge, dual carriageways now speed the motorist into Liverpool. Since the war many miles of dual carriage-way have been constructed to ease traffic-flow along the Liverpool–Southport, St. Helens–Ormskirk, Southport–Preston, Preston–Blackburn and many other roads, and the East Lancashire Road has been considerably improved by being made a dual carriageway throughout. A second Mersey Tunnel now joins Liverpool to Wallasey and to Wirral's motor roads, and all the bigger towns in Lancashire have implemented schemes for a freer flow of local and through traffic. Manchester has its Mancunian Way, Liverpool its flyovers, and such towns as Preston, Blackburn, Bolton, Salford, and St. Helens have built new links and by-passes as part of their 'urban renewal'.

Since the mid-1950s the railways have begun to challenge road transport again. They have closed down a few lines, but they have introduced nippy diesel services on several local routes, and, by offering parking facilities at local stations are encouraging commuters to travel to work by train. Above all they have electrified the main lines through the county, so that rail journeys from such places as Lancaster, Preston, Liverpool and Manchester to London, Glasgow, or Birmingham are very speedy indeed.

Ringway, albeit in Cheshire, is Lancashire's busiest airport. Speke, the second airport, does modest business especially in the holiday season, and Squires Gate has regular flights to other British and Irish airports. Warton and Samlesbury airfields are only used for aircraft testing, but periodically plans are proposed for bringing back into passenger service Burtonwood, the wartime trans-Atlantic terminal.

Excavating the tunnels at the Liverpool end of the Manchester-Liverpool Railway, 1828-30

Select Bibliography

Knowsley Hall Colonnade, 1732, at the South end of east wing

Items are arranged according to the order of chapters in the book. Titles of books are printed in italics; titles of articles are placed between inverted commas.

The following abbreviations are used:

V.C.H.	Victoria County History of Lancashire.
Ant. Soc.	Transactions of the Lancashire and Cheshire Antiquarian Society.
C.S.	Chetham Society Publications.
Hist. Soc.	Transactions of the Historic Society of Lancashire and Cheshire.
Rec. Soc.	Record Society of Lancashire and Cheshire Publications.

Watkins, W. T., *Roman Lancashire* (reprint 1969).

Shotter, D. C. A., *Romans in Lancashire* (1973).

Ant. Soc., 'Roman Fort at Castleshaw', Vols. 67, 71 and 77.

Hist. Soc., 'Roman Fort at Lancaster', Vol. 105; 'Roman Walton-le-Dale', Vol. 109.

Ekwall, E., *The Place Names of Lancashire* (1922).

Mills, D., *The Place Names of Lancashire* (1976).

Wainwright, F. T., *Scandinavian England* (1975). Reprints four major articles on Pre-Norman Lancashire.

V.C.H., Vol. 1, pp. 257-268; Vol. 2, pp. 1-8.

Collingwood, W. G., *Northumbrian Crosses of the Pre-Norman Age* (1927).

Ant. Soc., 'Pre-Conquest and Norman Churches', Vol. 60; Pre-Reformation Parishes', Vol. 67; 'Pre-Norman Churches of Old Heysham', Vol. 77.

V.C.H., 'Domesday Survey', Vol. 1.

Darby, H. C. and Maxwell, I. S., *The Domesday Geography of Northern England* (1962).

V.C.H., 'Religious Houses', Vol. 2.

Ashmore, O., *A Guide to Whalley Abbey* (1962).

Haigh, C., *The Last Days of the Lancashire Monasteries,* C.S., Vol. 17, 3rd series.

Webb, A. N., *Cartulary of Burscough Priory,* C.S., Vol. 18, 3rd series.

V.C.H., 'Political History', Vol. 2.

Hist. Soc., 'Roger of Poitou', Vol. 117.

Tupling, G. H., *Lancashire in the time of Edward II,* C.S., Vol. 1, 3rd series.

Holland, B., *The Lancashire Hollands* (1917).

Somerville, R., *History of the Duchy of Lancaster, 1265-1603* (1953).

Hist. Soc., 'Duchy and County Palatine', Vol. 103; 'Clerkship of the Peace', Vol. 106.

Shaw, R. C., *The Royal Forest of Lancaster* (1956).

Walker, F., *Historical Geography of S.W. Lancashire before the Industrial Revolution,* C.S., Vol. 103, new series.

Hist. Soc., 'Free Borough of Warrington', Vol. 105; articles on 'Common Fields', Vols. 113, 114 and 115.

Bagley, J. J. and Rowley P. B., *A Documentary History of England,* Vol. 1 (1966), contains the text of the Liverpool and Manchester borough charters.

Croston, J., *County Families of Lancashire and Cheshire* (1887).

V.C.H., 'Schools', Vol. 2.

Haigh, C., *Reformation and Resistance in Tudor Lancashire* (1975).

Halley, R., *Lancashire, its Puritanism and Noncomformity* (1872).

Bagley, J. J., *Lancashire Diarists* (1975).

Broxap, E., *The Great Civil War in Lancashire, 1642-51* (new edition 1973).

Dore, R. N., *The Great Civil War (1642-46) in the Manchester Area* (1973).

Ant. Soc., 'Wigan's Part in the Civil War, 1639-51', Vol. 47.

Jacobite Trials at Manchester, 1694 and *Lancashire Memorials of the Rebellion, 1715,* C.S., Vols. 28 and 5, old series.

Jarvis, R. C., Articles on 1745 Rebellion in Hist. Soc., Vols. 98 and 108, and Ant. Soc., Vols. 62 and 65.

Hist. Soc., 'John Lunt', Vol. 115; 'History of the Plague', Vol. 90; 'Sick Poor in the Seventeenth Century', Vol. 102; 'First House of Correction', Vol. 105; 'Household Inventories', Vol. 110; 'Plague, Poverty and Population', Vol. 112.

Bagley, J. J. and A. J., *The English Poor Law* (1966)—contains Lancashire examples.

Smith, L. T. (ed.), *The Itinerary of John Leland,*. Vols. 2, 4 and 5 (1906-10).

Camden, W., *Britannia* (1637 and later editions).

Morris, C., *The Journeys of Celia Fiennes* (1947).

Holt, *A General View of the Agriculture of the County of Lancashire* (1795).

Chandler, G., *William Roscoe of Liverpool* (1953).

Harley, J. B., *William Yates's Map of Lancashire, 1786* (1967).

Parkinson, C. N., *The Rise of the Port of Liverpool* (1952).

Muir, R., *A History of Liverpool* (new edition 1970).

Allison, J. E., *The Mersey Estuary* (1949).

Harris, J. R. (ed.), *Liverpool and Merserside* (1969).

Hist. Soc., 'Liverpool's First Dock', Vol. 93; 'Liverpool and the Slave Trade', Vol. 93; 'The Head Port of Chester', Vol. 102; 'Port of Chester', Vol. 117.

Anstey, R. and Hair, P. E. H. (ed.), *Liverpool, the African Slave Trade and Abolition* (1976).

Lowe, N., *The Lancashire Textile Industry in the Sixteenth Century*, C.S., Vol. 20, third series.

Wadsworth, A. P. and Mann, J. de L., *The Cotton Trade and Industrial Lancashire* (new edition 1965).

Ashmore, O., *Industrial Archaeology of Lancashire* (1969).

Aikin, J., *A Description of the Country round Manchester* (1795).

Mullineux, F., *The Duke of Bridgewater's Canal* (1959).

Hist. Soc., 'Liverpool–Prescot Turnpike', Vols. 88 and 89; 'Sankey Canal', Vol. 100; 'Lancashire Railways', Vol. 105; 'Colliery Railway', Vol. 114.

Nef, J. U., *The Rise of the British Coal Industry* (1932).

Harris, J. R., *The Copper King: a biography of Thomas Williams* (1964).

Barker, T. C., and Harris, J. R., *A Merseyside Town in the Industrial Revolution: St. Helens, 1750–1900* (1954).

Ant. Soc., 'Early Metal Trades', Vol. 61; 'Peel, Williams and Co.', Vol. 69; 'Factory Movement', Vol. 75–6.

Hist. Soc., 'Blundell's Collieries', Vols. 116, 117 and 119; 'Collier Girl', Vol. 120; 'Coal and Salt', Vol. 103.

Hardie, D. W. F., *A History of the Chemical Industry in Widnes* (1950).

Pink, W. D. and Beaven A., *The Parliamentary Representation of Lancashire, 1258–1885* (1899).

Hist. Soc., 'Gladstone in West Derby Hundred', and 'Preston Election of 1768', Vol. 111; 'Orator Hunt, M.P. for Preston', Vol. 114; 'Politics of Liverpool 1660–88', and 'Freemen Voter in Liverpool 1802–1835', Vol. 124.

Walmsley, R., *Peterloo: the Case reopened* (1969).

McCord, N., *The Activities and Organisation of the Anti-Corn-Law League.*

Frangopulo, N. J., *Rich Inheritance* (1963).

Bailey, F. A., *A History of Southport* (1955).

Eyre, K., *Seven Golden Miles* (new edition 1975).

Ant. Soc., 'Blackpool, 1740-1851', Vol. 69.

Hist. Soc., 'Morecambe, 1820–62', Vol. 100.

Millward, R., *Lancashire: the History of the Landscape* (1955).

Bell, S. P. (ed.), *Victorian Lancashire* (1974).

Hist. Soc., 'Local Boards of Health', Vol. 117. 'Life in East Lancashire', Vol. 120; 'Liverpool Court and Cellar Dwellings', Vol. 122.

Smith, W. (ed.), *A Scientific Survey of Merseyside* (1953).

Carter, C. F. (ed.), *Manchester and its Region* (1962).

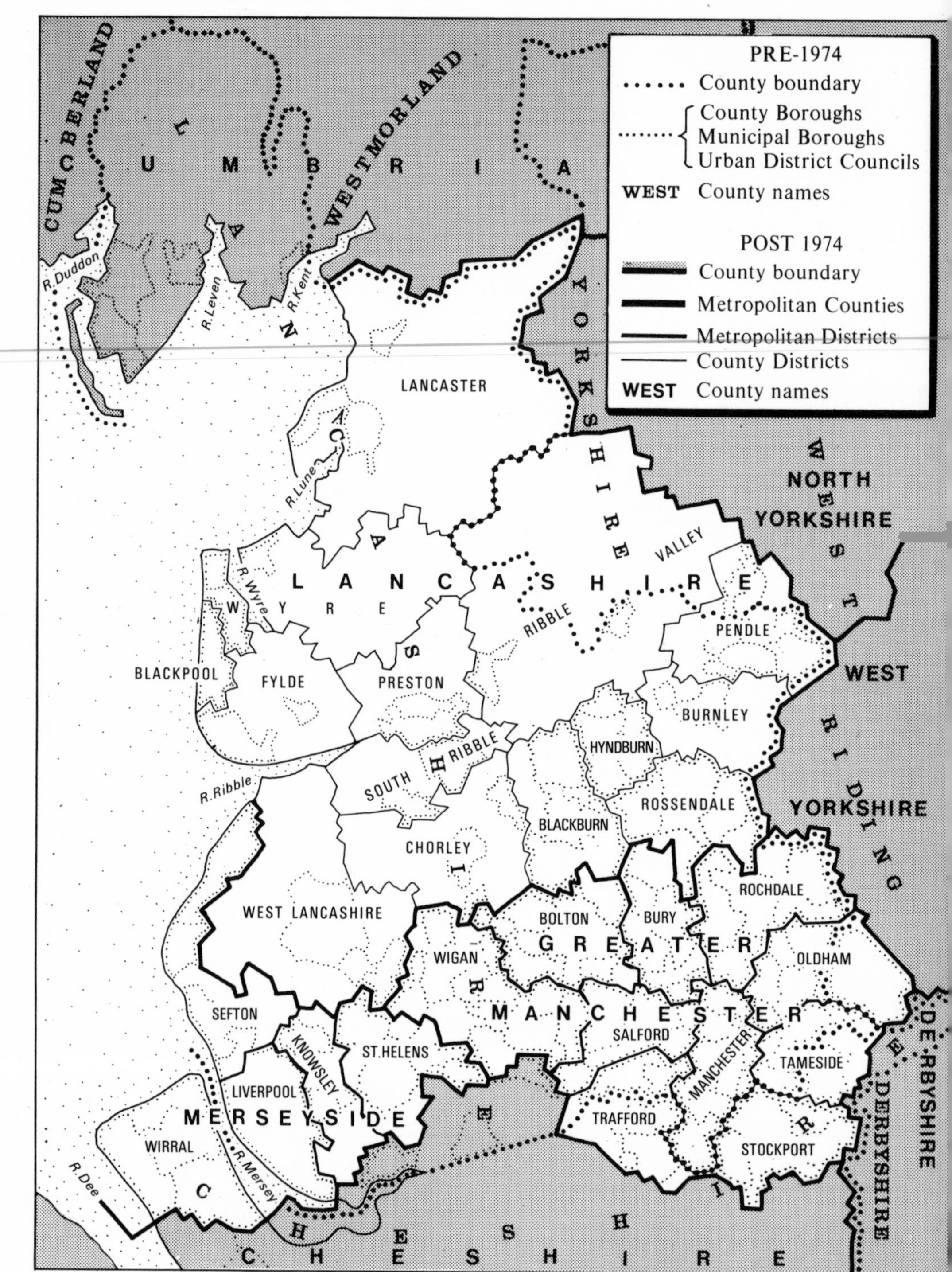

The Partition of Lancashire, April 1974

NOTE to map opposite.

Local Government reorganisation in 1974 reduced Lancashire drastically. The two new metropolitan counties, Merseyside and Greater Manchester, took huge bites out of the South West and South East, and Cheshire stepped across the Mersey to absorb Warrington and Widnes— the little the young giants had left of what had been South Lancashire.

In the north, the new Cumbria added Lancashire north of Morecambe Bay to the old counties of Westmorland and Cumberland, and the Lancashire-Yorkshire border was adjusted in Lancashire's favour to make it more 'rational'.

The result is that Lancashire, centred on Preston, now consists of little more than the middle third of the old county palatine.

Index